Table of Contents

List of Contributors

Centers for Disease Control and Prevention, National Institute for Occupational Safety and Health

Centers for Disease Control and Prevention, Office of Infectious Diseases

Centers for Disease Control and Prevention, Office of Public Health Preparedness and Response

National Security Staff, Legal Affairs Directorate

National Security Staff, Resilience Directorate

Office of Personnel Management

U.S. Agency for International Development

U.S. Department of Health & Human Services, National Institutes of Health

U.S. Department of Health & Human Services, Office of the General Counsel

U.S. Department of Health & Human Services, Food and Drug Administration

U.S. Department of Health & Human Services, Centers for Medicare & Medicaid Services

U.S. Department of Health & Human Services, Office of the Assistant Secretary for Preparedness and Response

U.S. Department of Agriculture, Office of the General Counsel

U.S. Department of Defense, Army Research Laboratory Survivability/Lethality Analysis Directorate

U.S. Department of Defense, Defense Threat Reduction Agency, J9 Research & Development

U.S. Department of Defense, Joint Chiefs of Staff, J4 Logistics Directorate

U.S. Department of Defense, Joint Chiefs of Staff, J5 Strategic Plans and Policy Directorate

U.S. Department of Defense, Office of the General Counsel

U.S. Department of Defense, Office of the Secretary of Defense, Office of the Assistant Secretary of Defense for Health Affairs

U.S. Department of Defense, Office of the Secretary of Defense, Office of the Assistant Secretary of Defense for Homeland Defense and Americas' Security Affairs

U.S. Department of Defense, Office of the Secretary of Defense, Director of OSD Cost Assessment and Program Evaluation

U.S. Department of Defense, Office of the Secretary of Defense, Office of the Under Secretary of Defense for Policy

U.S. Department of Homeland Security, Customs and Border Protection

U.S. Department of Homeland Security, Federal Emergency Management Agency

U.S. Department of Homeland Security, Office of Health Affairs

U.S. Department of Homeland Security, National Protection and Programs Directorate

U.S. Department of Homeland Security, Office of Policy

U.S. Department of Homeland Security, U.S. Coast Guard

U.S. Department of Homeland Security, U.S. Secret Service

U.S. Department of Justice, Office of Justice Programs

U.S. Department of Justice, Civil Division

U.S. Department of Justice, Federal Bureau of Investigation

U.S. Department of Justice, National Security Division

U.S. Department of Justice, Office of Foreign Litigation

U.S. Department of Labor, Occupational Safety & Health Administration

U.S. Department of State

U.S. Department of Transportation, National Highway Traffic Safety Administration, Office of Emergency Medical Services

U.S. Department of Transportation, Office of the Under Secretary for Policy

U.S. Department of Veterans Affairs, Veterans Health Administration Office of Emergency Management

Executive Summary

Recent improvised explosive device (IED) and active shooter incidents reveal that some traditional practices of first responders need to be realigned and enhanced to improve survivability of victims and the safety of first responders caring for them. This Federal, multi-disciplinary first responder guidance translates evidence-based response strategies from the U.S. military's vast experience in responding to and managing casualties from IED and/or active shooter incidents and from its significant investment in combat casualty care research into the civilian first responder environment. Additionally, civilian best practices and lessons learned from similar incidents, both in the United States and abroad, are incorporated into this guidance. Recommendations developed in this paper fall into three general categories: hemorrhage control, protective equipment (which includes, but is not limited to, ballistic vests, helmets, and eyewear), and response and incident management.

Hemorrhage Control

1. First responders should incorporate tourniquets and hemostatic agents as part of treatment for severe bleeding (if allowed by protocol). Tourniquets and hemostatic agents have been demonstrated to be quick and effective methods for preventing exsanguination from extremity wounds (tourniquets) and other severe external bleeding (hemostatic agents).

2. First responders should develop and adopt evidence-based standardized training that addresses the basic, civilianized tenets of Tactical Combat Casualty Care (TCCC). Training should be conducted in conjunction with fire, emergency medical services (EMS), and medical community personnel to improve interoperability during IED and/or active shooter incidents.

Protective Equipment

1. First responders should develop inter-domain (EMS, fire, and law enforcement) Tactics, Techniques, and Procedures (TTPs)—including use of ballistic vests, better situational awareness, and application of concealment and cover concepts—and train first responders on them.

2. As technology improves, first responders should adopt proven protective measures (e.g., body armor) that have been demonstrated to reliably shield personnel from IED fragments and shock waves.

3. First responders, when dealing with either IED or active shooter incidents, must remain vigilant and aware of the potential risk posed by secondary IEDs or additional shooters.

Response and Incident Management

1. Local and state law enforcement and emergency services should institutionalize National Incident Management System (NIMS)-based command and control language through plans and exercises and during ongoing education and training.

2. Local and state emergency management, EMS, fire, and law enforcement personnel and receiving medical facilities should have interoperable radio and communications equipment.

3. Local, state and federal partners should consider expansion of Public Safety Answering/Access Point (PSAP) intake procedures to include information gathering vital to the initial response.

4. Training to improve first responder triaging precision is essential for dealing with IED and/or active shooter incidents.

5. There should be greater coordination among EMS, fire services, and law enforcement to work more effectively during IED and/or active shooter incidents. The dialogue should focus on potential improvements or changes to the TTPs which have historically been used during law enforcement

situations that involve a medical emergency (e.g., EMS waits until law enforcement secures the scene before they enter to render emergency care).

The recommendations presented—early, aggressive hemorrhage control; use of body armor and a more integrated response; and greater first responder interoperability—will help to save lives by mitigating first responder risk and by improving the emergent and immediate medical management of casualties encountered during IED and/or active shooter incidents.

Purpose

Recent improvised explosive device (IED) and active shooter incidents reveal that some traditional practices of first responders need to be realigned and enhanced—with an emphasis on early hemorrhage control and a more integrated response by first responders (i.e., emergency medical services [EMS], fire, law enforcement, and rescue personnel)—to improve survivability of victims and the safety of first responders caring for them.[1] At the request of first responders and first receivers (e.g., medical technicians, nurses, and physicians) who have encountered mass casualties from IEDs and/or active shooter incidents, this document was developed to provide guidance on how to better approach these incidents.

Responders should also consider the combination of both IEDs and active shooter incidents in an organized, complex attack (such as the Mumbai attacks in 2008) that requires both treatment and extraction of the injured from a still-hostile environment. The conditions during such tactical assaults in a civilian setting speak to the need for first responders and first receivers to adopt evidence-based hemorrhage control, risk evaluation, and casualty management measures in a potentially dangerous environment.

As a result of these developments, the Department of Homeland Security, in coordination with the Department of Defense (DoD), Department of Health and Human Services, Department of Justice, Department of Transportation, White House Office of Science and Technology Policy, and the National Security Staff, has developed recommendations for individuals who provide emergent and immediate medical management of casualties resulting from IEDs and/or active shooter incidents. Based on best practices and lessons learned, this document focuses on the medical response to IEDs and/or active shooter incidents with recommendations for hemorrhage control, protective equipment (which includes ballistic vests, helmets, and eyewear), and response and incident management.

Background

A. Defining First Responders

In this guidance, the term "first responder" refers to a diverse set of persons who, from the earliest stages of an incident, are critical to managing and caring for people who are injured by an IED and/or active shooter incident. The term "first responder" does not imply a formal credential, certification, limitation, or capacity. First responders may include bystanders, law enforcement, and EMS and fire personnel. EMS and fire personnel typically encompass the traditional scopes of practice as identified in the National Highway Traffic Safety Administration's National Scope of Practice Model (2007). Levels of medical credentialing and quantity of resources for EMS and fire personnel can vary greatly depending on the EMS delivery model. Bystanders, who likely will be on scene prior to EMS, fire, or law enforcement arrival, may or may not have some form of medical training, and those volunteering at the site of an attack may be poorly equipped and at risk for additional explosions, ballistic threats, and hazardous environments. In some areas, the jurisdiction involved may benefit from volunteer services such as Community Emergency Response Teams (CERTs), the Emergency System for Advance Registration of Volunteer Health Professionals, or the Medical Reserve Corps (MRC). These volunteers are organized and trained to provide community support to natural disasters, accidents, and attacks. In the United States, the role of first receivers is frequently associated with "brick and mortar" medical facilities that often do not have the protective equipment necessary to face potential hostile conditions or hazardous environments.

B. Defining the Threat

Single or multiple IED events targeting civilians and/or first responders represent an ongoing and growing threat from domestic and foreign individuals or groups. In the United States between 1970 and 2011, excluding the 9/11 attacks, four of six attacks with more than 50 injuries, and 22 of 45 attacks with more than five injuries, involved IEDs.[2] IED "types" likely to cause mass casualties include "leave behind" parcels, backpacks, or luggage placed in crowded environments; "suicide vests" or "suicide belts"; and especially vehicle bombs. Traumatic injuries may result from IEDs in many ways: from penetration or blunt force trauma caused by the fragmentation and high-velocity projection of pieces of its immediate container (e.g., a metal pipe, box, or pressure cooker); from items intentionally added to compound the number of projectiles (e.g., ball bearing, nails, etc.); from incidental fragmentation and projection of material or debris from a larger container or vessel the IED is placed within (e.g., a vehicle trunk or trash bin); by collateral fragmentation and/or projection of material affected by blast, such as windows, walls, or other objects in the vicinity; and by blast overpressure itself, without any projectiles at all. Where an IED is placed—indoors or out, near or far from other objects—will influence its blast effects. Understanding the numerous ways in which IEDs can cause injuries and how the environment plays a role in exacerbating or mitigating their blast effects is critical to increasing survivability when unexploded IEDs are present or secondary IEDs are suspected. In addition to causing life and limb threatening injuries, these events generate confusion, uncertainty, and fear at the scene that ripple throughout the receiving medical system.

Active shooter incidents represent a similar, and increasing, threat to responders. Like IED events, active shooter incidents require extraordinary efforts on the part of first responders. Though these incidents typically end within a short period of time, some may involve large, complex locations and require many hours to clear suspected hazards after the initial event.

C.   Military Lessons Learned and Civilian Adaptation

Experience in combat casualty care gained by the U.S. military during the wars in Iraq and Afghanistan, augmented by the DoD's investment in trauma care and surgical research, has resulted in a vast amount of knowledge pertaining to the management of explosive injury and gunshot wounds, with a particular focus on life-threatening external hemorrhage control.

Tactical Combat Casualty Care

Information on wounds suffered by U.S. Army soldiers in Vietnam between July 1967 and June 1979 found that of those killed in action, 9 percent died from extremity hemorrhage, 5 percent died from tension pneumothorax, and 1 percent died from airway obstruction.[3] These findings, that one-sixth of combat casualties result from three types of wounds that are easily treated in the field, led to the development in the late 1990s of Tactical Combat Casualty Care (TCCC)—a set of prehospital trauma care guidelines for battlefield use that focus on the most common causes of treatable exsanguination deaths in combat.[4]

Tactical Emergency Casualty Care

Recognizing how this military experience could apply to civilian high-threat medical operations, an independent group of civilian first responders in 2011 founded the Committee for Tactical Emergency Casualty Care (C-TECC)[5] to develop guidelines that translate military medical lessons learned from the battlefield to civilian crisis response. The resulting Tactical Emergency Casualty Care (TECC) guidelines are a set of evidence-based best practice recommendations for casualty management during high-threat civilian tactical and rescue operations that are based on military TCCC principles but account for differences in the civilian environment, resources allocation, patient population, and scope of practice. It is important to emphasize that C-TECC is an independent civilian entity and not necessarily endorsed by the DoD. TECC is the civilian evolution of TCCC, written to address the subtle differences in the civilian operational environment.[6]

A collaborative group of public safety organizations—including fire, law enforcement, pre-hospital care, trauma care, and the military—convened in Hartford, Connecticut, in the spring of 2013 to develop consensus regarding strategies to increase survivability in mass-casualty shootings (commonly referred as the Hartford Consensus). The group states that "no one should die from uncontrolled bleeding" and developed the acronym THREAT to address these situations:

> Threat suppression,
> Hemorrhage control,
> Rapid Extrication to safety,
> Assessment by medical providers, and
> Transport to definitive care.[7]

In its "Call to Action," this group of experts advocates that uninjured or minimally injured victims can act as rescuers; law enforcement should utilize external hemorrhage control as a core skill; EMS, fire, and rescue response must be more fully integrated and their traditional role limitations revised; and existing trauma systems should be used to optimize seamless care.

Concerned international and national first responder associations, such as the International Association of Chiefs of Police, International Association of Fire Fighters, International Association of Fire Chiefs, National Association of Emergency Medical Technicians, and the National Tactical Officers Associations, have shown great interest in this topic, and many have published position statements. The fire associations state that "common tactics, common communications capabilities and a common lexicon for seamless, effective operations" [i] are required and "integrated and coordinated planning, policies, training and team building prior to the incident will ensure effective and successful response." [ii] Additionally, the National Tactical Officers Association (NTOA) states that there is a need for all police officers to have basic Tactical Emergency Medical Support (TEMS) medical training in order to potentially save the lives of victims, bystanders, police officers, and suspects in the event they are wounded.

NTOA has also stated that there is no single model for providing care during law enforcement operations and that TEMS basic principles should be considered core law enforcement skills relevant to all police operations, as NTOA "supports the efforts of the Committee for Tactical Emergency Casualty Care (C-TECC) and others to foster the development of standardized taxonomy and evidence based clinical practice guidelines tailored to the law enforcement mission." [iii]

The following is a list of select TCCC/TECC interventions that have potential applicability in civilian trauma care systems following an IED and/or active shooter event:

1. The use of tourniquets to control extremity hemorrhage.

2. The use of hemostatic gauze to control bleeding from sites not amenable to tourniquet.

3. The use of a nasopharyngeal airway for patients without maxillofacial or neck trauma.

4. Positioning of a casualty in a recovery posture if feasible for conscious patients with maxillofacial trauma and bleeding into the airway.

5. Spinal precautions when feasible for patients with blunt but not penetrating trauma.

6. Intravenous (IV) access is not routinely required in the initial phase of treatment but can be performed by those with appropriate training and oversight.

The following additional interventions may be performed by those with advanced life support (ALS) training and capabilities:

7. Surgical airway if "sit up and lean forward" posture not possible in those with face/neck trauma.

8. Intraosseous (IO) access for medications or fluids when IV not successful or possible IO access is not routinely required in the initial phase of treatment.

9. IV morphine, oral transmucosal fentanyl citrate lozenges, and ketamine for analgesia.

Lessons learned from the military's recent combat experiences, and their civilian C-TECC counterparts, are incorporated within this guidance.

En Route Care

It is important to emphasize that emergency medical care activities should not stop as a casualty is evacuated. In fact, the military's experience demonstrates that continuation or escalation of these measures is critical in

---

[i] *IAFF Position Statement: Active Shooter Events. http://www.iaff.org/Comm/PDFs/ IAFF_Active_Shooter_Position_Statement.pdf.*

[ii] *IAFC Position Statement: Active Shooter Events. http://www.iafc.org/files/1ASSOC/ IAFCPosition_ActiveShooterEvents.pdf.*

[iii] *TEMS Position Statement. http://ntoa.org/sections/tems/tems-position-statement/.*

reducing mortality during prehospital care. While there is a need to understand how these military experiences in prehospital patient care can be leveraged to decrease morbidity (illness or injury) and mortality (death) in the civilian setting, the ability to translate the military's findings related to on-site and en route care to the civilian setting has not been fully demonstrated.

Hospital-Based Measures

The military's combat casualty care research on hospital-based management of patients with severe explosion-related injuries is documented in a Balad Air Base Report from 2008[8] and on the Joint Trauma System Clinical Practice Guidelines website.[iv]

One particularly successful strategy is damage control resuscitation (DCR), which demonstrated decreased mortality associated with the use of a blood component-based volume replacement compared to the use of crystalloid fluids for patients in shock. DCR is based on the balanced administration of thawed plasma, pRBCs, and platelets in severely injured patients instead of solutions such as normal saline and lactated ringers.[9] [10] [11] [12] DCR also includes avoidance of hypothermia and pursuit of other measures to maximize oxygenation and reduce injurious factors in the blast-injured patient.

D.   Improvised Explosive Device Incidents

Morbidity and Mortality Prevention

There are three broad concepts related to the prevention or reduction of morbidity and mortality associated with an explosive event:

1. *Prevention:* Avoiding or thwarting the detonation is obviously the best way to avert IED-related injury, suffering, and death. Primary preventive measures, including improvements in preemptive mental health capabilities, an aware public who is able and willing to report suspicious pre-attack behaviors, tactical operations employed to render the device safe, and law enforcement intelligence gathering and threat-analysis capabilities, are beyond the scope of this paper. Preventing injuries of first responders and the public is of great importance. Safe distance from suspicious packages aids in preventing injuries from IEDs (see Figure 1).

2. *Mitigation:* This concept refers to actions taken to reduce the impact of an explosive event once an explosion has occurred, such as use of protective equipment and the placement of physical blast mitigation barriers or windows, and are sometimes referred to as secondary preventive measures. Some of the more sophisticated military protective equipment—including vests with ceramic plates, helmets, and protective undergarments—have been designed for and tested against mechanisms of injury resulting from explosive devices and ballistic threats. Most of the protective equipment available to civilian first responders, however, has been designed for protection from ballistic threats and was not designed, manufactured, or intended to provide protection from IEDs. It should also be noted that most protective equipment is focused on ballistic protection and may have unproven or limited value for mitigating fragmentation or blast overpressure, particularly for devices with larger net explosive weights, such as vehicle bombs. For protective equipment and barriers to be effective, they must be implemented proactively; they are of little use when the explosive event is random and enacted on an unsuspecting, unprotected group of individuals.

[iv] *http://www.usaisr.amedd.army.mil/cpgs.html.*

3. **Response:** This encompasses the initial treatment activities taken by first responders at the scene of injury and care provided while en route to the medical facility to prevent or reduce morbidity and mortality of individuals who have been injured by an explosive event.

BOMB THREAT STAND-OFF CARD

Threat Description	Explosives Capacity	Mandatory Evacuation Distance	Shelter-in-Place Zone	Preferred Evacuation Distance
Pipe Bomb	5 lbs	70 ft	71-1199 ft	+1200 ft
Suicide Bomber	20 lbs	110 ft	111-1699 ft	+1700 ft
Briefcase/Suitcase	50 lbs	150 ft	151-1849 ft	+1850 ft
Car	500 lbs	320 ft	321-1899 ft	+1900 ft
SUV/Van	1,000 lbs	400 ft	401-2399 ft	+2400 ft
Small Delivery Truck	4,000 lbs	640 ft	641-3799 ft	+3800 ft
Container/Water Truck	10,000 lbs	860 ft	861-5099 ft	+5100 ft
Semi-Trailer	60,000 lbs	1570 ft	1571-9299 ft	+9300 ft

Figure 1[v]

Published Civilian Experience

Civilian reports on the response to explosive incidents are primarily from non-U.S. centers and include those in Madrid, London, and Tel Aviv. [13][14][15][16][17][18][19] These, and a limited number of other reports, have provided valuable lessons learned regarding emergency response, triage, and surge requirements for an explosive incident. However, these studies provide little detail on prehospital, blood bank, operating room, health care provider, and hospital ward resource requirements following these events and are of limited applicability to emergency planning for similar events within the U.S. civilian sector.

Civilian response in the United States will vary depending on the geographic location, resources, and demographics of the incident. In most areas, the civilian response will be led by local law enforcement and emergency services. Routinely, requests for emergency assistance are obtained through Public Safety Answering/ Access Points (PSAP). The PSAP functions as the initial information collection point and can prove invaluable in coordinating the public sector response. Conversely, poor incident reporting and improperly dispatched response assets can lead to a delay in patient care.

[v] *DHS/DOJ, Bomb Threat Stand-Off Card, Washington DC, 2014.*

Responders to active shooter incidents at Virginia Tech and in Aurora and Columbine in Colorado encountered various access denial schemes in the form of chemical munitions, fire, secondary IEDs, and mechanical obstructions. International IED and concerted attacks have utilized fire, smoke, chemical (chlorine), and security elements to challenge first responders and increase the damage and effectiveness of the attack.

CDC guidelines provide general strategies for the U.S. health care system in the event of a civilian terrorist bombing.[20] These CDC guidelines also include next steps such as forecasting necessary blood bank, operating room, and other associated hospital infrastructure resources. The CDC has also developed and disseminated courses and guidelines that address both the patient care and health care system challenges of medical response to civilian terrorist bombings. These materials were informed by U.S. civilian experts in prehospital and hospital care relating to mass casualty response, the DoD military medical experience, and those who led medical responses to terrorist bombings in Israel, Pakistan, London, Madrid, Mumbai, and Delhi. This material, designated the Terrorism Injuries: Information, Dissemination and Exchange (TIIDE) project, is available through the TIIDE Project website.[vi]

E.   Active Shooter Incidents

Morbidity and Mortality Prevention

There are three broad concepts related to the prevention or reduction of morbidity and mortality associated with an active shooter incident:

1. *Prevention:* Avoiding or thwarting the active shooter incident is obviously the best way to avert active shooter-related injury, suffering, and death. Primary preventive measures, including improvements in preemptive mental health capabilities, an aware public who is able and willing to report suspicious pre-attack behaviors, and law enforcement active shooter intelligence gathering and threat-analysis capabilities, are beyond the scope of this paper.[21]

2. *Mitigation:* This concept refers to actions taken to reduce the impact of an active shooter incident: evaluation of acceptable risk to facilitate provision of medical care for victims as soon as possible; use of protective equipment, such as ballistic vests, appropriate to the threat; and development of first responder TTPs that focus on active shooter scenarios. Other mitigation actions, such as a public trained in active shooter response or victim initiated mitigation measures,[22] are outside of the scope of this paper.

3. *Response:* This encompasses the initial treatment activities taken by first responders at the scene of injury and care provided while en route to the medical facility to prevent or reduce morbidity and mortality of individuals who have been injured in an active shooter incident. Rapid first responder access to victims in an active shooter incident can make the difference between life and death, as the survival rate diminishes rapidly for seriously injured trauma victims the longer they must wait to receive definitive hospital care.[23]

Published Civilian Experience

Civilian reports on the response to active shooter incidents draw primarily from watershed domestic events such as the 1999 Columbine High School,[24] 2007 Virginia Tech,[25] and 2009 Fort Hood shootings,[26] as well as the 2008 Mumbai terrorist attacks.[27] Studies from these and other primarily domestic events have provided valuable lessons regarding active shooter incident response policy, victim treatment, and first responder protective

---

[vi] *http://www.amtrauma.org/?page=BlastPrimer.*

equipment recommendations. Lessons learned include concepts originally developed for and validated by the military during the conflicts in Iraq and Afghanistan that challenge some long-standing EMS principles of practice. Evaluation of these concepts seeks a balance between providing expeditious medical response for victims and ensuring effective risk management for first responder safety.

The current standard EMS response for an active shooter incident is to stage in a secure location until police mitigate the threat and secure the area. This can lead to a significant delay in providing medical care to the victims. Empirical evidence demonstrates that in an active shooter scenario, expeditious medical intervention, more than capability/capacity, was key to preventing loss of life.[28] Emerging alternatives to the "standby" policy suggest a level of first responder collaboration that allows EMS with appropriate protective equipment to quickly enter the incident scene with law enforcement officers in order to stabilize patients and reduce fatalities from readily treatable injuries. Variability exists in the training and deployment of law enforcement officers to rescue and care for victims. Law enforcement planners should employ strategies that enable all law enforcement officers to provide lifesaving care until additional resources can be moved forward.

Studies examining the weapons used during active shooter incidents, and the patterns of morbidity and mortality of these incidents, indicate that civilian active shooter scenarios present similar injuries and conditions to those seen in combat (in decreasing order of mortality): extremity hemorrhage, tension pneumothorax, or airway obstruction.[28] Each of these wounds is readily treatable with minimal supplies, but they are very time sensitive, and delay in treatment increases the risk of mortality. Because victims in an active shooter incident are more likely to suffer exsanguinating extremity wounds than airway injury, and because a person can bleed to death from a large arterial wound in 2-3 minutes while it may take 4-5 minutes to die from a compromised airway, C-TECC guidelines place control of external hemorrhage ahead of airway control—replacing the traditional ABC mnemonic (for airway, breathing, circulation) with MARCH (Massive hemorrhage control/Airway support/Respiratory threats/Circulation [prevent shock]/Hypothermia).

F.   Hemorrhage Control

Control of External Hemorrhage in the Prehospital Setting

Tourniquet use on the battlefield has been demonstrated to be effective in decreasing the number of treatable exsanguination deaths due to extremity hemorrhage. There are a variety of tourniquets in use at present by the U.S. military. A recent comprehensive study of U.S. combat fatalities from 2001 to 2011 noted that the incidence of treatable exsanguination deaths related to extremity hemorrhage dropped from 7.8 percent in a previous study[29] to 2.6 percent by 2011,[30] a decrease attributed to the implementation of tourniquet use by U.S. forces. The number of U.S. lives saved in combat through the use of tourniquets alone is estimated to be between 1,000 and 2,000.[31] To be most effective, the tourniquet must be applied before the victim has lost enough blood to suffer hemorrhagic shock. Despite previous warnings about limb ischemia, there was no preventable loss of limbs resulting from tourniquet ischemia in a case study of 232 patients with tourniquets on 309 extremities.[32]

> *A shift from the traditional mantra of "tourniquet as a last resort" to "tourniquets are proven to save lives from treatable exsanguination injuries" is supported by evidence and will necessitate interoperable training across all domains of EMS, fire, and law enforcement.*

Anatomic areas such as the neck, the groin, and the axilla contain large vascular structures and are not amenable to tourniquet placement. Studies at military medical research laboratories have evaluated the efficacy of hemostatic agents and found an advantage in the use of "packing hemostatic gauze" vs. granulated hemostatics. [33] [34] Junctional hemorrhage control devices such as the Combat Ready Clamp, the Abdominal Aortic Tourniquet, and the Junctional Emergency Treatment Tool may also be used to control hemorrhage from the groin area.

Direct pressure can also be used to control external bleeding, a technique that can work even with bleeding from major vessels such as the carotid or femoral arteries. Direct pressure must be applied consistently and with significant force to stop the bleeding and is best employed with the patient on a firm surface so that effective counterpressure is present. To control severe bleeding, direct pressure must be sustained until the casualty reaches an operating room, where surgical repair of the vessel can be performed.

Current guidelines and best practice recommendations for control of external hemorrhage and casualty management during civilian tactical and rescue operations are published on the C-TECC website.[vii] The TCCC guidelines, which are the genesis for the TECC guidelines, were designed for military use and can be found on the National Association of Emergency Medical Technicians website.[viii]

[vii] http://c-tecc.org/images/content/TECC_Guidelines_DEC_2014_update.pdf.

[viii] https://www.naemt.org/education/TCCC/guidelines_curriculum.

[ix] E.M. Bulger, et al. Prehospital Guidelines for External Hemorrhage Control. Prehospital Emergency Care. 2014. 18:163-173.

G.   Protective Equipment

Protective equipment (which includes ballistic vests, helmets, and eyewear) for both civilian first responders and the military is designed and tested according to anticipated threats, injury patterns, and existing technology. Historically, first responders have been primarily concerned with protective equipment to counter firearm and, to a certain extent, chemical, biological, radiological, and nuclear threats—not IEDs.

First Responders

The development of standards and the manufacturing of this protective equipment for first responders have only been available since the 1970s.[35][36] The 126 percent increase in police officer fatalities from 1966 to 1971 prompted the Department of Justice to develop and evaluate concealable soft body armor for daily use that would protect against ballistic threats while minimizing blunt trauma.[37][38] Handguns have historically been the most common threat to police officers,[39] but National Institute of Justice (NIJ) ballistic vest testing parameters follow trends in threats, and updated testing parameters are added based on new knowledge of vest performance and necessary test conditions.[40][41]

> *First responder adoption of inter-domain tactics, techniques, and procedures that include the use of ballistic vests, better situational awareness, and the application of concealment and cover concepts ultimately increases first responder safety and allows quicker access to victims resulting in improved patient outcomes.*

Currently there are five types of ballistic vests based on NIJ body armor standards. However, statistics from the Bulletproof Vest Partnership/Body Armor Safety Initiative[x] suggest that the majority of vests used by first responders are Type II and IIIA. Descriptions of the body armor standards are listed below, ordered by the level of protection. For instance, Type IIA provides protection against Type II and IIA threats, whereas Type III vests provide protection for Type IIA, Type II, and Type IIIA threats. All of the vests listed, with the exception of Types III and IV, are considered concealable body armor and designed to fit under a normal uniform shirt.[42] Some manufacturers also produce soft armor vests that accommodate "trauma packs", which are ballistic inserts added to a vest to provide added protection. These inserts are referred to as "in conjunction" designs and are similar to military ballistic inserts. These "in conjunction" designs must be threat level tested and labeled appropriately.[42] In other words, if a Type III vest provides Type III protection only in conjunction with a trauma pack, then the system's label must be marked accordingly. It is important to note that none of the five armor types have requirements to defeat IED fragments and therefore may not provide meaningful protection against either fragmentation or blast overpressure effects from IEDs. While other standards exist for protective suits used by public safety bomb technicians, the suits' weight, bulk, and limited numbers make them impractical for general use by first responders. The degree of protection civilian soft and rigid armors will provide against the complex shock and impact profiles that IEDs present is unknown. While available armor may provide some degree of protection from IED fragmentation, the fact it is unlikely to mitigate blast overpressure effects should be carefully considered by responders when involved in confirmed or suspected IED incidents, especially those in which larger net-explosive-weight IEDs such as vehicle bombs are confirmed or suspected.

---

[x] *http://www.ojp.usdoj.gov/bvpbasi.*

NIJ Standard-0101.06 establishes five formal armor classification types:[43] [44]

Type IIA	protects against 9 mm; .40 S&W
Type II	protects against 9 mm; .357 Magnum
Type IIIA	protects against.357 SIG; .44 Magnum
Type III	protects against Rifles; 7.62mm FMJ
Type IV	protects against Armor Piercing Rifles; .30 caliber AP

Army Testing of Personal Protective Equipment

Over the last several years, the U.S. Army Test and Evaluation Command (ATEC) has conducted thousands of ballistic tests of protective equipment, including individual pieces of equipment traditionally thought of as "body armor" (softer material vests containing hard armor plates), helmets, bomb suits, eye and face protection, extremity and pelvic protection, and concealable body armor. In a majority of these tests, the threats evaluated include 7.62mm to 9mm bullets, metallic fragments of various sizes and shapes, stab tests using both blade and pick threats, blast tests, and blunt trauma tests. Other types of testing are also conducted, such as durability, reliability, wearability, and suitability. Permission to review reports must be obtained from the test sponsor, since ATEC was contracted to conduct the assessment and is thus not the owner of the subsequent test data. All reports can be requested through the ATEC website.[xi]

H.   Response and Incident Management

The National Response Framework (NRF), which is built upon NIMS, describes the Nation's principles, roles and responsibilities, and coordinating structures for managing serious or large-scale incidents. Implementation of these elements, through training and education, helps mitigate risk by reinforcing the importance of unified command, interoperability, a standardized lexicon, and consideration of lessons learned from exercises and operations. Training and education on these elements also enable responders to adapt efficiently to evolving risks and allow for effective integration across all missions using a standards-based approach.

> *Greater collaboration and interoperability among EMS, fire services, and law enforcement during IED and/or active shooter events can save lives.*

NIMS promotes the use of a common operating picture, interoperability of communications, and information management as essential principles in incident management. The ability of first responders to communicate with voice and/or data across disciplines and jurisdictions is central to improving the efficiency and effectiveness of incident response and emergency management activities. During initial response, the PSAP plays a particularly important role as the initial information link between those at the incident scene and EMS, fire responders, and law enforcement.

The United States Fire Administration (USFA) advocates that EMS, fire, and law enforcement personnel quickly establish unified command at scenes of IED and active shooter incidents.[xii] EMS and fire personnel should be aware that law enforcement will aggressively and hastily send first arriving law enforcement personnel into the affected area of active shooter incidents to engage and neutralize the threat, to secure the perimeter to

---

[xi] *www.atec.army.mil/foia.html.*
[xii] *http://www.usfa.fema.gov/downloads/pdf/publications/active_shooter_guide.pdf.*

ensure the perpetrator does not escape, and to prevent inappropriate entry into the scene. The first arriving law enforcement personnel focused on neutralizing active shooter threats will typically not stop to render aid to injured bystanders, as the top priority is to stop further harm by addressing the threat. EMS and fire personnel, upon arrival to the scene, should move to the law enforcement command post, establish unified command as previously planned and exercised with law enforcement personnel, and anticipate active involvement in warm zone operations. A warm zone is an area of indirect threat, where law enforcement has either cleared or isolated the threat to a level of minimal or mitigated risk. This area can be considered clear but not secure.[xiii]

The USFA also advocates that EMS, fire, and law enforcement personnel must ensure that there are common tactics, communication capabilities, protocols, and procedures that are well practiced, exercised and known by all emergency services personnel before an IED and/or active shooter event occurs. The protocols and procedures should also address non-traditional roles of EMS and fire personnel. These roles include the use of properly trained, armored (not armed) medical personnel who are accompanied by law enforcement into areas of mitigated risk (warm zones). In these roles, life-saving care (i.e., hemorrhage control and airway management) and evacuation of the injured from the warm zone may help improve survivability of victims..[xv]

Incorporation of EMS and fire into warm zones, where it is practiced, is at the discretion of the jurisdiction and is dependent on resources and relationships between all involved parties. There are various models and approaches for introducing EMS and fire personnel into warm zones, including the Rescue Task Force (RTF) model.[xvi xvii] RTFs, under the protection of law enforcement officers, render emergent and life-saving treatment at the basic life support level, stabilization, and removal of the injured victims of IED and/or active shooter incidents while wearing recommended ballistic protective equipment. Some RTF models include the use of one ALS provider per RTF, and other non-RTF models include the exclusive use of law enforcement for rapid patient removal of injured victims to awaiting EMS personnel in areas more distant from the threat, but still within the warm zone. Whichever model is used, the treatment rendered in the warm zone is limited to basic, urgent life-saving care focused on severe hemorrhage control and airway management.

Law enforcement agencies should train personnel to provide casualty care to establish a lifesaving bridge to victims at an active shooter incident. Based on the immediacy of the threat and the geographic location of victims, law enforcement officers providing casualty care may offer the best chance for victim survival. Law enforcement programs that have robust rescue capabilities should train with supporting EMS programs and develop patient transfer measures that optimize patient survivability. A select few models have EMS and/or fire personnel accompanying the law enforcement personnel into active (hot) zones. Regardless of the model adopted, the calculated and early incorporation of properly trained personnel (EMS, fire, and/or law enforcement) into warm zones allows critically injured victims to receive life-saving care in a more-timely manner.

Rendering life-saving care in warm zones (by EMS, fire, and/or law enforcement) is a relatively new paradigm that is supported by data. Historically, when EMS and fire personnel waited up to several hours before being permitted to enter scenes and render life-saving care, very few critical victims survived. The passage of that time resulted in the likely preventable loss of life for victims. The Wound Data and Munitions Effectiveness Team showed that 90 percent of Vietnam deaths occurred prior to definitive care, with 42 percent occurring within 5 to

[xiii] http://www.iafc.org/files/1ASSOC/IAFCPosition_ActiveShooterEvents.pdf.
[xiv] http://www.iaff.org/Comm/PDFs/IAFF_Active_Shooter_Position_Statement.pdf.
[xv] http://www.usfa.fema.gov/downloads/pdf/publications/active_shooter_guide.pdf.
[xvi] http://www.usfa.fema.gov/downloads/pdf/publications/active_shooter_guide.pdf.
[xvii] http://www.iaff.org/Comm/PDFs/IAFF_Active_Shooter_Position_Statement.pdf.

30 minutes of injury.[xvii] Although the combat setting is not a direct translation into the civilian setting, the fact that most of the 42 percent of deaths were related to exsanguination from extremity wounds should be considered when deciding to incorporate trained personnel (EMS, fire, and/or law enforcement) into the scene to render life-saving hemorrhage control and airway management sooner rather than later.

Greater interoperability and collaborative education and training among EMS, fire services, and law enforcement during IED and/or active shooter events will enable first responders to conduct well-integrated and effective incident response and emergency management that can ultimately save more lives.

[xviii] *Wound Data and Munitions Effectiveness Team. The WDMET Study, Bethesda; Uniformed Services University of the Health Sciences; 1970.*

Responder Guidelines

The following guidelines for addressing hemorrhage control, protective equipment, and response and incident management were developed by the Federal Government through a collaborative evaluation of lessons learned from both military and civilian experience in reducing morbidity and mortality following an IED and/or active shooter incident.

A.   Hemorrhage Control

1. *First responders should incorporate tourniquets and hemostatic agents as part of treatment for severe bleeding (if allowed by protocol).*

Tourniquets and hemostatic agents have been demonstrated to be quick and effective methods for preventing exsanguination from extremity wounds (tourniquets) and other severe external bleeding (hemostatic agents). First responders should update training and educational content on tourniquets and hemostatic agents into a consistent standard within EMS, fire, and law enforcement domains.

2. *First responders should adopt, develop training for, and operationalize the evidence-based guidelines of TECC. Training should be conducted in conjunction with EMS, fire, law enforcement, and medical community personnel to improve interoperability during IED and/or active shooter events.*

In order for the training to be most effective, it should be conducted from a systems perspective, involving EMS, fire, and law enforcement. This practice promotes better interoperability between EMS, fire, and law enforcement during IED and/or active shooter incidents, with the ultimate goal of saving lives.[45]

B.   Protective Equipment

1. *First responders should develop inter-domain (EMS, fire, and law enforcement) TTPs—including use of ballistic vests, better situational awareness, and application of concealment and cover concepts—and train first responders on proper use of the TTPs.*

The incorporation of ballistic vests and the concepts of concealment and cover into the EMS and fire professions, when active shooter threats and situations warrant, will better protect first responders. Additionally, the TTPs will facilitate improved interoperability between EMS and fire personnel and law enforcement during active shooter incidents.

2. *As technology improves, first responders should adopt protective measures (e.g., body armor) proven to shield personnel from IED fragments and shock waves.*

At the time of this publication, the body armor currently used by most civilian personnel may not protect against fragmentation or blast overpressure effects from IEDs. Further research on the effectiveness of protective equipment in IED incidents is, and should remain, on-going. The first responder community should adopt recommendations for improved protection as they become available.

3. *First responders must remain vigilant and aware of secondary devices or additional shooters when dealing with either IED or active shooter incidents.*

First responders should routinely conduct collaborative training and exercises on response to IED and/or active shooter events and take into consideration the possible presence of secondary devices and additional shooters. In addition to continual situational awareness of the scene, appropriate protective equipment, including ballistic vests, should be considered by all responders on the scene. EMS, fire, and law enforcement personnel should employ standardized TTPs and consistent training to promote interoperability during IED and/or active shooter events, with the understanding that there is not yet evidence to support the effectiveness of protective equipment for IED hazards.

C. Response and Incident Management

1. Local and state law enforcementand emergency services, should institutionalize NIMS-based command and control language and plans and exercises through ongoing education and training.

Civilian response programs should develop joint policies, training, tactics, and communications that enhance the interoperability of all of the emergency services team (EMS, fire, emergency management, law enforcement, and others). Further information regarding NIMS and the NRF is available on the FEMA website.[xix][xx]

2. Local and state emergency management, EMS, fire, law enforcement and receiving medical facilities should have interoperable radio and communications equipment.

Clear, concise communications and scene coordination between law enforcement and emergency services should be regularly tested through collaborative training and exercises. First responders should have the ability to talk across disciplines and jurisdictions via radio communications systems, exchanging voice and/or data with one another on demand, in real time, when needed, and as authorized. Law enforcement and emergency services leadership should explore when, where, and how to set up incident command posts, emergency operations centers, and briefing locations that are safe and secure from attempts to disrupt communications.

3. Local, state and federal partners need to consider expansion of PSAP intake procedures to include information gathering vital to the initial response.

The PSAP is the initial information link between those at the incident scene and EMS and law enforcement responders. Development of joint PSAP, intake, dispatch, and communications plans, along with a common lexicon, will enhance first responder interoperability throughout all phases of these incidents.

4. Training to improve first responder triaging precision and decrease unnecessary transport delays is essential for dealing with IED and/or active shooter incidents.

Patients should be triaged for both priority of transport and for the destination. Under-triage can result in potentially life threatening conditions going unrecognized, resulting in delayed transport or transport to an inappropriate facility, while over-triaging risks having lower acuity patients overwhelm limited resources in higher-level medical facilities that could be better utilized treating more severely injured patients. With proper triage, the right patient will get to the right facility in the right time. First responders should routinely practice triage with a consideration for both medical priority of transport and capabilities of the destination treatment facility to maintain competency with the skill and knowledge.

5. There should be greater coordination among EMS, fire services, and law enforcement to work more effectively during IED and/or active shooter incidents. The dialogue should focus on potential improvements or changes to the TTPs that have historically been used during law enforcement situations that involve a medical emergency (i.e., EMS waits until law enforcement secures the scene before they enter to render emergency care)

[xix] *http://www.fema.gov/national-incident-management-system.*
[xx] *http://www.fema.gov/national-response-framework.*

The dialogue should focus on a mutual understanding of how the various first responder components approach IED and/or active shooter response operations, where areas of improvements and synergy might be found, and how evidence based clinical data and outcomes can be incorporated into future standards, education, and training. This may result in significant cultural and operational changes that contradict current practices.

EMS, fire, and law enforcement personnel must ensure that common tactics, communication capabilities, protocols, and procedures are well practiced, exercised, and known by all emergency services personnel before an IED and/or active shooter event occurs.. The protocols and procedures should also address non-traditional roles of EMS and fire personnel, including in warm zone operations, as previously described.

There are various models and approaches for introducing EMS and fire personnel into warm zones, as detailed earlier in this document. Regardless of the model adopted by the local jurisdiction, the calculated and early incorporation of properly trained EMS, fire, and law enforcement personnel into warm zones allows critically injured victims to receive life-saving care in a more timely manner.

Summary

This multi-disciplinary first responder guidance is the first of its kind to link the categories of prevention against IEDs and/or active shooter incidents to tangible, evidence-based response strategies designed to mitigate morbidity and mortality. This document builds on the U.S. military's vast experience in responding to and managing casualties from IEDs and/or active shooter incidents and on its significant investment in combat casualty care research, then filters it through civilian peer review literature and consensus-based best practices to distill practical, proven guidelines for effectively responding to these devastating events.

Current military practice and experience emphasize early and definitive control of external hemorrhage and have been estimated to have saved up to 2,000 American lives in Iraq and Afghanistan. Although the significance of life-threatening hemorrhage in civilian mass casualty has not been as clearly defined as it has in the military combat setting, until further data shows the need for a different medical emphasis, hemorrhage control should remain a priority. As such, aspects of this military experience have been translated to a number of civilian medical systems around the Nation. However, permeation of military and international lessons learned in the arena of medical response to explosive injury and/or active shooter incidents is incomplete. In most cases, the research conducted on protective equipment by the U.S. military can be translated to the civilian setting to assist in better protecting the workforce of first responders who are called upon to respond to IED and/or active shooter incidents. The focus on interoperability improvements between emergency services domains (EMS, fire, and law enforcement) will aid in saving lives impacted by IED and/or active shooter incidents.

To prepare for and reduce death and suffering following an IED detonation and/or active shooter event in a civilian environment, it is imperative that more widespread dissemination and adoption of lessons learned from these incidents, as well as the DoD's continuing combat medicine experience, occur within the U.S. civilian first responder and first receiver communities.

Threat-Based Scenarios

This section includes a list of scenarios and recommended medical and planning considerations. As the end-users of these scenarios, first responders are encouraged to incorporate details relevant to their local landmarks, response procedures, and practices. The purpose of the following scenarios is to guide first responder education and training efforts toward incorporation and institutionalization of the previous responder guidelines in a variety of likely IED and/or active shooter situations. These scenarios can be used individually as stand-alone resources, or they can be used in conjunction with the other scenarios provided. They are intended to be used for collaborative planning, training, and exercises with EMS, fire, and law enforcement resources together. Ideally, role playing should be done to help first responders better understand each other's processes and roles and the importance of unified command and interoperability.

Scenario 1: Large-Scale Terrorist/Insurgency Attack

Scenario 2: Medium-Scale Terrorist/Insurgency Attack

Scenario 3: Medium-Scale Terrorist/Insurgency Attack

Scenario 4: Small Scale Attack

Scenario 5: Unwitting Suicide Bomber

Scenario 6: Discovery/Recovery of Homemade Explosives (Not an Attack)

Scenario 7: Active Shooter with Access Denial to First Responders

Scenario 8: Active Shooter in a Public Commercial Facility

Scenario 9: Active Shooter in an Open, Outdoor, Unbounded Location

Scenario 10: Active Shooter in a Public Sports Complex

Scenario 1: Large-Scale Terrorist/Insurgency Attack

Large-scale attack using an IED with over 100 pounds net explosive weight, producing mass casualties with the likelihood of overwhelming the response and receiving infrastructure. This scenario may include vehicle-borne improvised explosive devices (VBIEDs).

EXAMPLE: You are called to the scene of a reported explosion at a train station (or other public location). Initial reports indicate that a truck drove around barriers and into the entrance of the facility and then detonated. 911 callers indicate that there are several dead and many others with multiple injuries—some extremely serious. You are the first arriving unit on the scene...

Expected Injury Patterns

For those who survive this event, injuries can include multiple amputees with pelvic/perineal components, penetrating thoraco-abdominal injuries, pulmonary contusions from closed space blasts, burns, TBI, including penetrating head injury, and neck trauma. While primary blast injuries can occur from both open space (e.g., roadside IED) and closed space (e.g., buildings, trains, and buses) bombings, it is especially common after closed space bombings.

Protective Equipment and Barriers

Secondary preventive measures include activities to prevent injuries once an explosion has occurred. Such measures may include barrier or structural walls that may protect or reduce injuries to bystanders and responders from blast and fragmentation injuries.[xxi] Secondary preventive measures also include use of ballistic protective equipment, although soft body armor and ceramic plate body armor may not protect against fragmentation or blast overpressure effects from IEDs. Most protective equipment is focused on ballistic protection and may have unproven or limited value for mitigating fragmentation or blast overpressure, particularly for devices with larger net explosive weights, such as vehicle bombs. For protective equipment and barriers to be effective, they must be implemented proactively; they are of little use when the explosive event is random and enacted on an unsuspecting, unprotected group of individuals. Ballistic protective equipment will also give some level of protection should an IED attack be combined with an active shooter event. Experience indicates attackers may plan to detonate secondary or subsequent IEDs that target first responders or receiving hospitals.

First responders should consider wearing some level of ballistic protective equipment. Considerations for first responder ballistic protective equipment should include what type of equipment is best suited for EMS and fire responders and when it should be worn (every shift, during times of high risk [e.g., on duty at a sports stadium], or just in response to IED events). It is critical that incident commanders base protective equipment and tactical movement guidance at the incident scene on a situational assessment of the IED risk, particularly when IEDs with significant net explosive weight are suspected or confirmed to be present. These types of IEDs, including vehicle bombs, may produce blast overpressure effects that would not be mitigated by typical protective equipment or available cover. A false sense of security among first responders could result if net explosive weight

---

[xxi] *Blast injuries are the result of the rapid chemical conversion of a solid or liquid into highly pressurized gasses that expand rapidly and compress the surrounding air. This generates a pressure pulse, which spreads as a blast wave in all directions. The effects of the blast wave are more intense in a confined space like a building or bus. The shock wave is amplified as it is reflected off walls, floors, and the ceiling. If the blast occurs outside, the blast wave will dissipate rapidly. It is understood that over-pressure phenomena may enhance the lethality of blast effect for explosions that occur in confined spaces.*

is not considered when determining protective equipment or tactical movement guidance to responders.

Protective Equipment Commonly Worn

Most law enforcement officers responding to the incident will be wearing Type II or IIIA bullet resistant vests, designed to stop bullets from most handguns, and shotgun pellets. Given the expected injuries, this level of protective equipment may not provide protection from blast overpressure and fragmentation, and extremities will be vulnerable. First responders other than law enforcement typically do not wear ballistic protective equipment. Civilians at public places will not be wearing any form of ballistic protective equipment.

Protective Equipment Risk Mitigation Considerations

The NIJ body armor standard specifies the ballistic threats that body armor must reliably protect against. This standard does not specify a requirement for ballistic resistant vests to protect against fragmentation threats. The Type II or IIIA ballistic resistant vests that law enforcement officers are most commonly issued will likely not protect against fragmentation and blast overpressure effects from an IED threat. Use of Type IV body armor may increase the probability of protection against fragmentation and blast overpressure. However, further research and development is required to validate the performance of NIJ-approved body armor against fragmentation threats and to provide guidance on what level of protection should be worn to respond to this type of IED event.

Response and Incident Management Considerations

Maximize interoperability through existing MOUs/MOAs/SOPs, as well as through frequent exercises, planning, and training. These efforts will ultimately aid in reducing time from injury to treatment. During response, and while on the scene of the incident, use unified command with a mutual understanding of each responder's role (EMS, fire, and law enforcement). Strive to communicate on common frequencies and use standardized terminology. Ensure all responders (regardless of discipline—EMS, fire, and law enforcement) are trained and equipped to provide early, aggressive hemorrhage control; use protective equipment (which includes ballistic vests, helmets, and eyewear); and use integrated response and incident management.

Medical Response System

An IED detonation has the potential of instantly producing hundreds of casualties (there were over 700 casualties after the Oklahoma City bombing) with injuries that range across the entire spectrum of severity. A system-wide medical response to this event should be well-coordinated, incorporating the lessons learned from the military (both system and individual patient care) and experiences from domestic and international bombings. Unlike the management of routine emergencies, the response to IED incidents will be extraordinary for the Nation's trauma and EMS systems.

System-wide efforts should include activities ranging from self-care, buddy-care, and bystander care to proper and effective prehospital triaging and patient transport to get the right patients to the appropriate medical facilities in a swift and orderly manner, regardless of proximity. The efforts include prehospital emergency medical services, ground ambulances, rotary and fixed wing aircraft patient transport, designated trauma centers, hospitals, and rehabilitation facilities.

Prehospital Emergency Medical Services Considerations

Patient-Based Considerations: The last decade of war has seen significant advances in the ability of prehospital care to impact the mortality of combat wounds. The ability to stop life-threatening bleeding from extremity wounds has been demonstrated to reduce the number of treatable exsanguination deaths.

As IEDs have become a common source of wounding in the wars in Iraq and Afghanistan, and as the use of IEDs in the United States (the Boston Marathon bombing on April 15, 2013) has become a reality, civilian adoption of some military clinical practices that are a significant departure from traditional prehospital care should be considered:

- Aggressive hemorrhage control—including use of tourniquets and, where appropriate, hemostatic agents
- Aggressive airway management, including "sit up and lean forward" airway positioning
- Training all first responders in self-care, buddy care, and bystander care

System-Wide Implications

Experience from bombings occurring in other countries demonstrates common prehospital care system challenges, including multiple simultaneous attacks that cause an enormous number of casualties that exceed the available resources of EMS responders. The adoption of techniques that are suitable for use in self-care, buddy-care, bystander care, and care delivered by first responders is essential to extend the depth of responders available to provide immediate life-saving care.

EMS must rapidly and accurately triage casualties at the incident site and expeditiously transport those identified for "immediate care" into an appropriate hospital setting. It is imperative that pre-hospital triaging of wounded patients be as efficient and accurate as possible. Over-triage of patients over-taxes specialty centers that are designed to care for more significantly injured patients, while under-triaging of patients puts critically wounded patients into facilities that may not be able to provide the life-saving care needed. In addition to proper triage, care must be taken to regulate the transportation of casualties in order to direct victims to the hospital best suited for providing the necessary level of care for the type and severity of injuries they have sustained. Often the closest hospital is quickly overwhelmed by injured transported by ambulances, police cars, and privately owned vehicles, as well as the "walking wounded". Because the influx of patients to the nearest hospital is dictated by human behavior outside control of the system, the EMS system must recognize this likelihood and plan for redistribution of injured patients such that the closest hospital can return to maximum functionality as soon as possible. Incident managers should also anticipate the need to provide for safety and security with the arrival of injured persons' family members, the "psychologically shocked," and the media.

EMS providers must also be cognizant of patients who appear otherwise well (uninjured), but may have traumatic brain injuries, tympanic membrane damage, and/or internal hollow organ damage due to the blast effects of the explosion. These considerations should be reinforced through exercise, planning, protocols, and training.

Hospital-Based Trauma System Considerations

Hospital challenges experienced in foreign and domestic bombings include:

- Difficulty in acquiring information from the scene
- Maldistribution of patients (e.g., two of 15 hospitals receiving approximately 60 percent of casualties from the scene in one large-scale event)
- A requirement for large numbers of hospital medical personnel to adequately treat the wounded
- The need to implement mass casualty contingency plans at every point of care (e.g., radiology postponing imaging an ankle sprain to rule out a fracture)

- Concern that the hospital may be a target
- Activation of Mass Transfusion Protocols, based on scope of injuries
- Activation of staff augmentation/call back plans, based on scope of injuries
- Initiation of patient movement/transfer plans, based on scope of injuries

Medical leaders of responses to bombings have noted that in many cases the majority of the injured and dead from large events present at the hospital closest to the scene. Patients able to leave the scene may forego EMS triage and present at hospitals before more severely injured patients arrive. The large influx of patients may exceed the hospital's capability to provide care, resulting in a "functional collapse" from inability to meet the demand spike. When this occurs, there is a compelling need to redistribute patients.

Distribution of patients among hospitals, so that no one hospital exceeds its resources, is a key principle in addressing medical surge capacity following bombing attacks that result in significant casualties.

To address the large number of patients arriving at local facilities, local hospitals will need the swift assistance of incoming health care providers to assist with re-triage of the arriving casualties and the provision of appropriate services to patients. This influx will include additional doctors, nurses, medical specialists, such as blood bank technologists and respiratory therapists, mental health providers, and chaplains. In addition, there will likely be the need for law enforcement personnel to maintain order and security. In the hours immediately after the blast, these additional personnel will likely come from surrounding communities and may include health care professionals from beyond the local area. While pre-event planning for cross-town (local) hospital credentialing and privileging of responding health care professionals can be arranged with relative ease, the issue of expeditious out-of-state credentialing and privileging of medical professionals responding to natural or man-made disasters can be more challenging.

Patient Movement/Transfer Considerations

As the patient load builds at local hospitals, some of the critically injured patients should be moved to other medical care facilities to optimize patient care. This will include movement to Level-1 trauma centers and other hospitals to better balance inpatient bed, operating room, intensive care unit, and rehabilitation bed utilization. Depending on the locality of the blast, this may include moving patients to other communities or across state lines. Long-distance transport of acutely injured patients will likely require aeromedical evacuation capabilities.

Scenario 2: Medium-Scale Terrorist/Insurgency Attack

Medium-scale attack using an IED with between 5 and 100 pounds net explosive weight, producing a significant number of mass casualties with the potential of overwhelming the response and receiving infrastructure. This scenario may include vehicle-borne improvised explosive devices (VBIEDs).

EXAMPLE: You are called to respond to an explosion inside a large house of worship in your response area. The 911 center received multiple calls, and there are many reported deaths and significant injuries. Your unit is the first arriving unit to the scene...

Expected Injury Patterns

For those who survive this event, injuries can include single and double amputees, extremity vascular injuries, penetrating foreign body thoraco-abdominal injuries, potential TBI and penetrating head trauma, neck trauma, and pulmonary contusions from closed space blasts.

Protective Equipment and Barriers

Secondary preventive measures include activities to prevent injuries once an explosion has occurred. Such measures may include barrier or structural walls that may protect or reduce injuries to bystanders and responders from blast and fragmentation injuries.[xxii] Secondary preventive measures also include use of ballistic protective equipment, although soft body armor and ceramic plate body armor may not protect against fragmentation or blast overpressure effects from IEDs. Most protective equipment is focused on ballistic protection and may have unproven or limited value for mitigating fragmentation or blast overpressure, particularly for devices with larger net explosive weights, such as vehicle bombs. For protective equipment and barriers to be effective, they must be implemented proactively; they are of little use when the explosive event is random and enacted on an unsuspecting, unprotected group of individuals. Ballistic protective equipment will also give some level of protection should an IED attack be combined with an active shooter event. Experience indicates attackers may plan to detonate secondary or subsequent IEDs that target first responders or receiving hospitals.

First responders should consider wearing some level of ballistic protective equipment. Considerations for first responder ballistic protective equipment should include what type of equipment is best suited for EMS and fire responders and when it should be worn (every shift, during times of high risk [e.g., on duty at a sports stadium], or just in response to IED events). It is critical that incident commanders base protective equipment and tactical movement guidance at the incident scene on a situational assessment of the IED risk, particularly when IEDs with significant net explosive weight are suspected or confirmed to be present. These types of IEDs, including vehicle bombs, may produce blast overpressure effects that would not be mitigated by typical protective equipment or available cover. A false sense of security among first responders could result if net explosive weight is not considered when determining protective equipment or tactical movement guidance to responders.

[xxii] Blast injuries are the result of the rapid chemical conversion of a solid or liquid into highly pressurized gasses that expand rapidly and compress the surrounding air. This generates a pressure pulse, which spreads as a blast wave in all directions. The effects of the blast wave are more intense in a confined space like a building or bus. The shock wave is amplified as it is reflected off walls, floors, and the ceiling. If the blast occurs outside, the blast wave will dissipate rapidly. It is understood that over-pressure phenomena may enhance the lethality of blast effect for explosions that occur in confined spaces.

Protective Equipment Commonly Worn

Most law enforcement officers responding to the incident will be wearing Type II or IIIA bullet resistant vests, designed to stop bullets from most handguns, and shotgun pellets. Given the expected injuries, this level of protective equipment may not provide protection from blast overpressure and fragmentation, and extremities will be vulnerable. First responders other than law enforcement typically do not wear ballistic protective equipment. Civilians at public places will not be wearing any form of ballistic protective equipment.

Protective Equipment Risk Mitigation Considerations

The NIJ body armor standard specifies the ballistic threats that body armor must reliably protect against. This standard does not specify a requirement for ballistic resistant vests to protect against fragmentation threats. The Type II or IIIA ballistic resistant vests that law enforcement officers are most commonly issued will likely not protect against fragmentation and blast overpressure effects from an IED threat. Use of Type IV body armor may increase the probability of protection against fragmentation and blast overpressure. However, further research and development is required to validate the performance of NIJ-approved body armor against fragmentation threats and to provide guidance on what level of protection should be worn to respond to this type of IED event.

Response and Incident Management Considerations

Maximize interoperability through existing MOUs/MOAs/SOPs, as well as through frequent exercises, planning, and training. These efforts will ultimately aid in reducing time from injury to treatment. During response, and while on the scene of the incident, use unified command with a mutual understanding of each responder's role (EMS, fire, and law enforcement). Strive to communicate on common frequencies and use standardized terminology. Ensure all responders (regardless of discipline—EMS, fire, law enforcement) are trained and equipped to provide early, aggressive hemorrhage control; use protective equipment (which includes ballistic vests, helmets, and eyewear); and use integrated response and incident management.

Medical Response System

An IED detonation has the potential of instantly producing hundreds of casualties (there were over 700 casualties after the Oklahoma City bombing) with injuries that range across the entire spectrum of severity. A system-wide medical response to this event should be well-coordinated, incorporating the lessons learned from the military (both system and individual patient care) and experiences from domestic and international bombings. Unlike the management of routine emergencies, the response to IED incidents will be extraordinary for the Nation's trauma and EMS systems.

System-wide efforts should include activities ranging from self-care, buddy-care, and bystander care to proper and effective prehospital triaging and patient transport to get the right patients to the appropriate medical facilities in a swift and orderly manner, regardless of proximity. The efforts include prehospital emergency medical services, ground ambulances, rotary and fixed wing aircraft patient transport, designated trauma centers, hospitals, and rehabilitation facilities.

Prehospital Emergency Medical Services Considerations

Patient-Based Considerations: The last decade of war has seen significant advances in the ability of prehospital care to impact the mortality of combat wounds. The ability to stop life-threatening bleeding from extremity wounds has been demonstrated to reduce the number of treatable exsanguination deaths.

As IEDs have become a common source of wounding in the wars in Iraq and Afghanistan, and as the use of IEDs in the United States (the Boston Marathon bombing on April 15, 2013) has become a reality, civilian adoption of some military clinical practices that are a significant departure from traditional prehospital care should be considered:

- Aggressive hemorrhage control—including use of tourniquets and, where appropriate, hemostatic agents
- Aggressive airway management, including "sit up and lean forward" airway positioning
- Training all first responders in self-care, buddy care, and bystander care

System-Wide Implications

Experience from bombings occurring in other countries demonstrates common prehospital care system challenges, including multiple simultaneous attacks that cause an enormous number of casualties that exceed the available resources of EMS responders. The adoption of techniques that are suitable for use in self-care, buddy-care, bystander care, and care delivered by first responders is essential to extend the depth of responders available to provide immediate life-saving care.

EMS must rapidly and accurately triage casualties at the incident site and expeditiously transport those identified for "immediate care" into an appropriate hospital setting. It is imperative that pre-hospital triaging of wounded patients be as efficient and accurate as possible. Over-triage of patients over-taxes specialty centers that are designed to care for more significantly injured patients, while under-triaging of patients puts critically wounded patients into facilities that may not be able to provide the life-saving care needed. In addition to proper triage, care must be taken to regulate the transportation of casualties in order to direct victims to the hospital best suited for providing the necessary level of care for the type and severity of injuries they have sustained. Often the closest hospital is quickly overwhelmed by injured transported by ambulances, police cars, and privately owned vehicles, as well as the "walking wounded". Because the influx of patients to the nearest hospital is dictated by human behavior outside control of the system, the EMS system must recognize this likelihood and plan for redistribution of injured patients such that the closest hospital can return to maximum functionality as soon as possible. Incident managers should also anticipate the need to provide for safety and security with the arrival of injured persons' family members, the "psychologically shocked," and the media.

EMS providers must also be cognizant of patients who appear otherwise well (uninjured), but may have traumatic brain injuries, tympanic membrane damage, and/or internal hollow organ damage due to the blast effects of the explosion. These considerations should be reinforced through exercise, planning, protocols, and training.

Hospital-Based Trauma System Considerations

Hospital challenges experienced in foreign and domestic bombings include:
- Difficulty in acquiring information from the scene
- Maldistribution of patients (e.g., two of 15 hospitals receiving approximately 60 percent of casualties from the scene in one large-scale event)
- A requirement for large numbers of hospital medical personnel to adequately treat the wounded
- The need to implement mass casualty contingency plans at every point of care (e.g., radiology postponing imaging an ankle sprain to rule out a fracture)
- Concern that the hospital may be a target
- Activation of Mass Transfusion Protocols, based on scope of injuries

- Activation of staff augmentation/call back plans, based on scope of injuries
- Initiation of patient movement/transfer plans, based on scope of injuries

Medical leaders of responses to bombings have noted that in many cases the majority of the injured and dead from large events present at the hospital closest to the scene. Patients able to leave the scene may forego EMS triage and present at hospitals before more severely injured patients arrive. The large influx of patients may exceed the hospital's capability to provide care, resulting in a "functional collapse" from inability to meet the demand spike. When this occurs, there is a compelling need to redistribute patients.

Distribution of patients among hospitals so that no one hospital exceeds its resources is a key principle in addressing medical surge capacity following terrorist bombings.

To address the large number of patients arriving at local facilities, local hospitals will need the swift assistance of incoming health care providers to assist with re-triage of the arriving casualties and the provision of appropriate services to patients. This influx will include additional doctors, nurses, medical specialists, such as blood bank technologists and respiratory therapists, mental health providers, and chaplains. In addition, there will likely be the need for law enforcement personnel to maintain order and security. In the hours immediately after the blast, these additional personnel will likely to come from surrounding communities and may require health care professionals from beyond the local area. While pre-event planning for cross-town (local) hospital credentialing and privileging of responding health care professionals can be arranged with relative ease, the issue of expeditious out-of-state credentialing and privileging of medical professionals responding to natural or man-made disasters can be more challenging.

Patient Movement/Transfer Considerations

As the patient load builds at local hospitals, some of the critically injured patients should be moved to other medical care facilities to optimize patient care. This will include movement to Level-1 trauma centers and other hospitals to better balance inpatient bed, operating room, intensive care unit, and rehabilitation bed utilization. Depending on the locality of the blast, this may include moving patients to other communities or across state lines. Long-distance transport of acutely injured patients will likely require aeromedical evacuation capabilities.

Scenario 3: Medium-Scale Terrorist/Insurgency Attack

Medium-scale attack using an IED with between 5 and 25 pounds net explosive weight. IEDs of this size frequently are placed in backpacks, suitcases, or buried and used to attack targets such as transportation infrastructure or specific locations to cause mass casualties with a potential of overwhelming the response and receiving infrastructure. This scenario includes suicide vest type devices that may be masked through clothing. Targets range from assassinations to mass casualties.

EXAMPLE: You are called to the scene of an explosion on a bus in your town center. A city bus full of passengers pulled into a crowded stop before exploding. You are the first arriving unit onto the scene...

Expected Injury Patterns

For those who survive this event, the injuries can include single and double amputees, extremity vascular injuries, penetrating foreign body thoraco-abdominal injuries, potential TBI and penetrating head trauma, neck trauma, and pulmonary contusions from closed space blasts.

Protective Equipment and Barriers

Secondary preventive measures include activities to prevent injuries once an explosion has occurred. Such measures may include barrier or structural walls that may protect or reduce injuries to bystanders and responders from blast and fragmentation injuries.[xxiii] Secondary preventive measures also include use of ballistic protective equipment, although soft body armor and ceramic plate body armor may not protect against fragmentation or blast overpressure effects from IEDs. Most protective equipment is focused on ballistic protection and may have unproven or limited value for mitigating fragmentation or blast overpressure, particularly for devices with larger net explosive weights, such as vehicle bombs. For protective equipment and barriers to be effective, they must be implemented proactively; they are of little use when the explosive event is random and enacted on an unsuspecting, unprotected group of individuals. Ballistic protective equipment will also give some level of protection should an IED attack be combined with an active shooter event. Experience indicates attackers may plan to detonate secondary or subsequent IEDs that target first responders or receiving hospitals.

First responders should consider wearing some level of ballistic protective equipment. Considerations for first responder ballistic protective equipment should include what type of equipment is best suited for EMS and fire responders and when it should be worn (every shift, during times of high risk [e.g., on duty at a sports stadium], or just in response to IED events). It is critical that incident commanders base protective equipment and tactical movement guidance at the incident scene on a situational assessment of the IED risk, particularly when IEDs with significant net explosive weight are suspected or confirmed to be present. These types of IEDs, including vehicle bombs, may produce blast overpressure effects that would not be mitigated by typical protective equipment or available cover. A false sense of security among first responders could result if net explosive weight is not considered when determining protective equipment or tactical movement guidance to responders.

[xxii] *Blast injuries are the result of the rapid chemical conversion of a solid or liquid into highly pressurized gasses that expand rapidly and compress the surrounding air. This generates a pressure pulse, which spreads as a blast wave in all directions. The effects of the blast wave are more intense in a confined space like a building or bus. The shock wave is amplified as it is reflected off walls, floors, and the ceiling. If the blast occurs outside, the blast wave will dissipate rapidly. It is understood that over-pressure phenomena may enhance the lethality of blast effect for explosions that occur in confined spaces.*

Protective Equipment Commonly Worn

Most law enforcement officers responding to the incident will be wearing Type II or IIIA bullet resistant vests, designed to stop bullets from most handguns, and shotgun pellets. Given the expected injuries, this level of protective equipment may not provide protection from blast overpressure and fragmentation, and extremities will be vulnerable. First responders other than law enforcement typically do not wear ballistic protective equipment. Civilians at public places will not be wearing any form of ballistic protective equipment.

Protective Equipment Risk Mitigation Considerations

The NIJ body armor standard specifies the ballistic threats that body armor must reliably protect against. This standard does not specify a requirement for ballistic resistant vests to protect against fragmentation threats. The Type II or IIIA ballistic resistant vests that law enforcement officers are most commonly issued will likely not protect against fragmentation and blast overpressure effects from an IED threat. Use of Type IV body armor may increase the probability of protection against fragmentation and blast overpressure. However, further research and development is required to validate the performance of NIJ-approved body armor against fragmentation threats and to provide guidance on what level of protection should be worn to respond to this type of IED event.

Response and Incident Management Considerations

Maximize interoperability through existing MOUs/MOAs/SOPs, as well as through frequent exercises, planning, and training. These efforts will ultimately aid in reducing time from injury to treatment. During response, and while on the scene of the incident, use unified command with a mutual understanding of each responder's role (EMS, fire, and law enforcement). Strive to communicate on common frequencies and use standardized terminology. Ensure all responders (regardless of discipline—EMS, fire, law enforcement) are trained and equipped to provide early, aggressive hemorrhage control; use protective equipment (which includes ballistic vests, helmets, and eyewear); and use integrated response and incident management.

Medical Response System

An IED detonation has the potential of instantly producing hundreds of casualties (there were over 700 casualties after the Oklahoma City bombing) with injuries that range across the entire spectrum of severity. A system-wide medical response to this event should be well-coordinated, incorporating the lessons learned from the military (both system and individual patient care) and experiences from domestic and international bombings. Unlike the management of routine emergencies, the response to IED incidents will be extraordinary for the Nation's trauma and EMS systems.

System-wide efforts should include activities ranging from self-care, buddy-care, and bystander care to proper and effective prehospital triaging and patient transport to get the right patients to the appropriate medical facilities in a swift and orderly manner. The efforts include prehospital emergency medical services, ground ambulances, rotary and fixed wing aircraft patient transport, designated trauma centers, hospitals, and rehabilitation facilities.

Prehospital Emergency Medical Services Considerations

Patient-Based Considerations: The last decade of war has seen significant advances in the ability of prehospital care to impact the mortality of combat wounds. The ability to stop life-threatening bleeding from extremity wounds has been demonstrated to reduce the number of treatable exsanguination deaths.

As IEDs have become a common source of wounding in the wars in Iraq and Afghanistan, and as the use of IEDs in the United States (the Boston Marathon bombing on April 15, 2013) has become a reality, civilian adoption of some military clinical practices that are a significant departure from traditional prehospital care is appropriate:

- Aggressive hemorrhage control—including use of tourniquets and, where appropriate, hemostatic agents
- Aggressive airway management, including "sit up and lean forward" airway positioning
- Training all first responders in self-care, buddy care, and bystander care

System-Wide Implications

Experience from terrorist bombings occurring in other countries demonstrates common prehospital care system challenges, including multiple simultaneous attacks that cause an enormous number of casualties that exceed the available resources of EMS responders. The adoption of techniques that are suitable for use in self-care, buddy-care, bystander care, and care delivered by first responders is essential to extend the range of persons providing immediate life-saving care.

EMS must rapidly and accurately triage casualties at the incident site and expeditiously transport those identified for "immediate care" into an appropriate hospital setting. It is imperative that pre-hospital triaging of wounded patients be as efficient and accurate as possible. Over-triage of patients over-taxes specialty centers that are designed to care for more significantly injured patients, while under-triaging of patients puts critically wounded patients into facilities that may not be able to provide the life-saving care needed. In addition to proper triage, care must be taken to regulate the transportation of casualties in order to direct victims to the hospital best suited for providing the necessary level of care for the type and severity of injuries they have sustained. Often the closest hospital is quickly overwhelmed by injured transported by ambulances, police cars, and privately owned vehicles, as well as the "walking wounded". Because the influx of patients to the nearest hospital is dictated by human behavior outside control of the system, the EMS system must recognize this likelihood and plan for redistribution of injured patients such that the closest hospital can return to maximum functionality as soon as possible. Incident managers should also anticipate the need to provide for safety and security with the arrival of injured persons' family members, the "psychologically shocked," and the media.

Hospital-Based Trauma System Considerations

Hospital challenges experienced in foreign and domestic bombings include:

- Difficulty in acquiring information from the scene
- Maldistribution of patients (e.g., two of 15 hospitals receiving approximately 60 percent of casualties from the scene in one large-scale event)
- A requirement for large numbers of hospital medical personnel to adequately treat the wounded
- The need to implement mass casualty contingency plans at every point of care (e.g., radiology postponing imaging an ankle sprain to rule out a fracture)
- Concern that the hospital may be a target
- Activation of Mass Transfusion Protocols, based on scope of injuries
- Activation of staff augmentation/call back plans, based on scope of injuries
- Initiation of patient movement/transfer plans, based on scope of injuries

Medical leaders of responses to bombings have noted that in many cases the majority of the injured and dead from large events present at the hospital closest to the scene. Patients able to leave the scene may forego EMS triage and present at hospitals before more severely injured patients arrive. The large influx of patients may exceed the hospital's capability to provide care, resulting in a "functional collapse" from inability to meet the demand spike. When this occurs, there is a compelling need to redistribute patients.

Distribution of patients among hospitals so that no one hospital exceeds its resources is a key principle in addressing medical surge capacity following bombing attacks that result in a significant number of casualties.

To address the large number of patients arriving at local facilities, local hospitals will need the swift assistance of incoming health care providers to assist with re-triage of the arriving casualties and the provision of appropriate services to patients. This influx will include additional doctors, nurses, medical specialists, such as blood bank technologists and respiratory therapists, mental health providers, and chaplains. In addition, there will likely be the need for law enforcement personnel to maintain order and security. In the hours immediately after the blast, these additional personnel will likely to come from surrounding communities and may require health care professionals from beyond the local area. While pre-event planning for cross-town (local) hospital credentialing and privileging of responding health care professionals can be arranged with relative ease, the issue of expeditious out-of-state credentialing and privileging of medical professionals responding to natural or man-made disasters can be more challenging.

Patient Movement/Transfer Considerations

As the patient load builds at local hospitals, some of the critically injured patients should be moved to other medical care facilities to optimize patient care. This will include movement to Level-1 trauma centers and other hospitals to better balance inpatient bed, operating room, intensive care unit, and rehabilitation bed utilization. Depending on the locality of the blast, this may include moving patients to other communities or across state lines. Long-distance transport of acutely injured patients will likely require aeromedical evacuation capabilities.

Scenario 4: Small Scale Terrorist/Insurgency Attack

Small-scale attack using an IED with less than 5 pounds net explosive weight. Assumed victim distance is 5 feet or less from center of the explosion. Use of high-energy explosives such as C-4 will cause smaller fragments traveling at higher velocity. Low-energy explosives, such as black powder filler in a pipe bomb, will generally result in larger fragments, which do not travel as far or fast. Oftentimes these small-scale attacks are targeted one-on-one events, and detonation occurs prior to first responder arrival.

EXAMPLE: You are called to the private residence for a reported explosion. One occupant of the house said his mother received and opened a package which detonated. There are two reported victims whose conditions are unknown. The caller was on the other side of the house when the explosion occurred...

Expected Injury Patterns

For those who survive this event, injuries can include digit and single amputees, soft tissue injuries, burns, ocular and tympanic injuries.

Protective Equipment and Barriers

Secondary preventive measures include activities to prevent injuries once an explosion has occurred. Such measures may include barrier or structural walls that may protect or reduce injuries to bystanders and responders from blast and fragmentation injuries.[xxiv] Secondary preventive measures also include use of ballistic protective equipment, although soft body armor and ceramic plate body armor may not protect against fragmentation or blast overpressure effects from IEDs. Most protective equipment is focused on ballistic protection and may have unproven or limited value for mitigating fragmentation or blast overpressure, particularly for devices with larger net explosive weights, such as vehicle bombs. For protective equipment and barriers to be effective, they must be implemented proactively; they are of little use when the explosive event is random and enacted on an unsuspecting, unprotected group of individuals. Ballistic protective equipment will also give some level of protection should an IED attack be combined with an active shooter event. Experience indicates attackers may plan to detonate secondary or subsequent IEDs that target first responders or receiving hospitals.

First responders should consider wearing some level of ballistic protective equipment. Considerations for first responder ballistic protective equipment should include what type of equipment is best suited for EMS and fire responders and when it should be worn (every shift, during times of high risk [e.g., on duty at a sports stadium], or just in response to IED events). It is critical that incident commanders base protective equipment and tactical movement guidance at the incident scene on a situational assessment of the IED risk, particularly when IEDs with significant net explosive weight are suspected or confirmed to be present. These types of IEDs, including vehicle bombs, may produce blast overpressure effects that would not be mitigated by typical protective equipment or available cover. A false sense of security among first responders could result if net explosive weight is not considered when determining protective equipment or tactical movement guidance to responders.

[xxiv] *Blast injuries are the result of the rapid chemical conversion of a solid or liquid into highly pressurized gasses that expand rapidly and compress the surrounding air. This generates a pressure pulse, which spreads as a blast wave in all directions. The effects of the blast wave are more intense in a confined space like a building or bus. The shock wave is amplified as it is reflected off walls, floors, and the ceiling. If the blast occurs outside, the blast wave will dissipate rapidly. It is understood that over-pressure phenomena may enhance the lethality of blast effect for explosions that occur in confined spaces.*

Protective Equipment Commonly Worn

Most law enforcement officers responding to the incident will be wearing Type II or IIIA bullet resistant vests, designed to stop bullets from most handguns, and shotgun pellets. Given the expected injuries, this level of protective equipment may not provide protection from blast overpressure and fragmentation, and extremities will be vulnerable. First responders other than law enforcement typically do not wear ballistic protective equipment. Civilians at public places will not be wearing any form of ballistic protective equipment.

Protective Equipment Risk Mitigation Considerations

The NIJ body armor standard specifies the ballistic threats that body armor must reliably protect against. This standard does not specify a requirement for ballistic resistant vests to protect against fragmentation threats. The Type II or IIIA ballistic resistant vests that law enforcement officers are most commonly issued will likely not protect against fragmentation and blast overpressure effects from an IED threat. Use of Type IV body armor may increase the probability of protection against fragmentation and blast overpressure. However, further research and development is required to validate the performance of NIJ-approved body armor against fragmentation threats and to provide guidance on what level of protection should be worn to respond to this type of IED event.

Response and Incident Management Considerations

Maximize interoperability through existing MOUs/MOAs/SOPs, as well as through frequent exercises, planning, and training. These efforts will ultimately aid in reducing time from injury to treatment. During response, and while on the scene of the incident, use unified command with a mutual understanding of each responder's role (EMS, fire, and law enforcement). Strive to communicate on common frequencies and use standardized terminology. Ensure all responders (regardless of discipline—EMS, fire, law enforcement) are trained and equipped to provide early, aggressive hemorrhage control; use protective equipment (which includes ballistic vests, helmets, and eyewear); and use integrated response and incident management.

Medical Response System

Smaller explosives, such as with this scenario, present with response challenges and resource demands, but are not as taxing to the medical system as a larger IED. Response to this event would be well-coordinated, incorporating the lessons learned from the military (both system and individual patient care) and experiences from domestic and international bombings. Unlike the management of routine emergencies, the response to IED incidents will be extraordinary for the Nation's trauma and EMS systems.

System-wide efforts should include activities ranging from self-care, buddy-care, and bystander care to proper and effective prehospital triaging and patient transport to get the right patients to the appropriate medical facilities in a swift and orderly manner. The efforts include prehospital emergency medical services, ground ambulances, rotary and fixed wing aircraft patient transport, designated trauma centers, hospitals, and rehabilitation facilities.

Prehospital Emergency Medical Services Considerations

Patient-Based Considerations: The last decade of war has seen significant advances in the ability of prehospital care to impact the mortality of combat wounds. The ability to stop life-threatening bleeding from extremity wounds has been demonstrated to reduce the number of treatable exsanguination deaths.

As IEDs have become a common source of wounding in the wars in Iraq and Afghanistan, and as the use of IEDs in the United States (the Boston Marathon bombing on April 15, 2013) has become a reality, civilian adoption of some military clinical practices that are a significant departure from traditional prehospital care is appropriate:

- Aggressive hemorrhage control—including use of tourniquets and, where appropriate, hemostatic agents
- Aggressive airway management, including "sit up and lean forward" airway positioning
- Training all first responders in self-care, buddy care, and bystander care

System-Wide Implications

Experience from bombings occurring in other countries demonstrates common prehospital care system challenges, including multiple simultaneous attacks that cause an enormous number of casualties that exceed the available resources of EMS responders. The adoption of techniques that are suitable for use in self-care, buddy-care, bystander care, and care delivered by first responders is essential to extend the range of persons providing immediate life-saving care.

EMS must rapidly and accurately triage casualties at the incident site and expeditiously transport those identified for "immediate care" into an appropriate hospital setting. It is imperative that pre-hospital triaging of wounded patients be as efficient and accurate as possible. Over-triage of patients over-taxes specialty centers that are designed to care for more significantly injured patients, while under-triaging of patients puts critically wounded patients into facilities that may not be able to provide the life-saving care needed. In addition to proper triage, care must be taken to regulate the transportation of casualties in order to direct victims to the hospital best suited for providing the necessary level of care for the type and severity of injuries they have sustained. Often the closest hospital is quickly overwhelmed by injured transported by ambulances, police cars, and privately owned vehicles, as well as the "walking wounded". Because the influx of patients to the nearest hospital is dictated by human behavior outside control of the system, the EMS system must recognize this likelihood and plan for redistribution of injured patients such that the closest hospital can return to maximum functionality as soon as possible. Incident managers should also anticipate the need to provide for safety and security with the arrival of injured persons' family members, the "psychologically shocked," and the media.

EMS providers must also be cognizant of patients who appear otherwise well (uninjured), but may have traumatic brain injuries, tympanic membrane damage, and/or internal hollow organ damage due to the blast effects of the explosion. These considerations should be reinforced through exercise, planning, protocols, and training.

Hospital-Based Trauma System Considerations

Hospital challenges experienced in foreign and domestic bombings include:

- Difficulty in acquiring information from the scene
- Maldistribution of patients (e.g., two of 15 hospitals receiving approximately 60 percent of casualties from the scene in one large-scale event)
- A requirement for large numbers of hospital medical personnel to adequately treat the wounded
- The need to implement mass casualty contingency plans at every point of care (e.g., radiology postponing imaging an ankle sprain to rule out a fracture)
- Concern that the hospital may be a target
- Activation of Mass Transfusion Protocols, based on scope of injuries

- Activation of staff augmentation/call back plans, based on scope of injuries
- Initiation of patient movement/transfer plans, based on scope of injuries

Medical leaders of responses to bombings have noted that in many cases the majority of the injured and dead from large events present at the hospital closest to the scene. Patients able to leave the scene may forego EMS triage and present at hospitals before more severely injured patients arrive. The large influx of patients may exceed the hospital's capability to provide care, resulting in a "functional collapse" from inability to meet the demand spike. When this occurs, there is a compelling need to redistribute patients.

Distribution of patients among hospitals so that no one hospital exceeds its resources is a key principle in addressing medical surge capacity following bombing attacks that result in a significant number of casualties.

To address the large number of patients arriving at local facilities, local hospitals will need the swift assistance of incoming health care providers to assist with re-triage of the arriving casualties and the provision of appropriate services to patients. This influx will include additional doctors, nurses, medical specialists, such as blood bank technologists and respiratory therapists, mental health providers, and chaplains. In addition, there will likely be the need for law enforcement personnel to maintain order and security. In the hours immediately after the blast, these additional personnel will likely come from surrounding communities and may require health care professionals from beyond the local area. While pre-event planning for cross-town (local) hospital credentialing and privileging of responding health care professionals can be arranged with relative ease, the issue of expeditious out-of-state credentialing and privileging of medical professionals responding to natural or man-made disasters can been more has challenging.

Patient Movement/Transfer Considerations

As the patient load builds at local hospitals, some of the critically injured patients should be moved to other medical care facilities to optimize patient care. This will include movement to Level-1 trauma centers and other hospitals to better balance inpatient bed, operating room, intensive care unit, and rehabilitation bed utilization. Depending on the locality of the blast, this may include moving patients to other communities or across state lines. Long-distance transport of acutely injured patients will likely require aeromedical evacuation capabilities.

Scenario 5: Involuntary Suicide Bomber

This category of IED attack involves a subject who is forced to wear a suicide vest or carry an explosive device with between 5 and 25 pounds net explosive weight to attack targets such as critical infrastructure, mass gatherings or specific individuals. This scenario includes suicide vest type devices that may be masked through clothing. Targets range from assassinations to mass casualties. Assumed target victim distance is 5-10 feet from center of the explosion. Victims (targets and/or unwitting suicide bomber) will not likely have protective equipment.

EXAMPLE: You are called to a packed movie theater for a distressed subject. Upon arrival, you are met by a terrified looking individual standing in the theater lobby who has a locked suicide vest on his chest. He says that if the demands on the piece of paper he has are not met, the vest that is secured to his chest will be detonated by the men who wrote the letter. He starts approaching you and begs you to help him... The movie theater is packed and the patrons inside are unaware that the man has a suicide vest on him...

Expected Injury Patterns

For those who survive this event, single and double amputees, extremity vascular injuries, penetrating foreign body thoraco-abdominal injuries, potential TBI and penetrating head trauma, neck trauma, and pulmonary contusions from closed space blasts.

Protective Equipment and Barriers

Secondary preventive measures include activities to prevent injuries once an explosion has occurred. Such measures may include barrier or structural walls that may protect or reduce injuries to bystanders and responders from blast and fragmentation injuries.[xxv] Secondary preventive measures also include use of ballistic protective equipment, although soft body armor and ceramic plate body armor may not protect against fragmentation or blast overpressure effects from IEDs. Most protective equipment is focused on ballistic protection and may have unproven or limited value for mitigating fragmentation or blast overpressure, particularly for devices with larger net explosive weights, such as vehicle bombs. For protective equipment and barriers to be effective, they must be implemented proactively; they are of little use when the explosive event is random and enacted on an unsuspecting, unprotected group of individuals. Ballistic protective equipment will also give some level of protection should an IED attack be combined with an active shooter event. Experience indicates attackers may plan to detonate secondary or subsequent IEDs that target first responders or receiving hospitals.

First responders should consider wearing some level of ballistic protective equipment. Considerations for first responder ballistic protective equipment should include what type of equipment is best suited for EMS and fire responders and when it should be worn (every shift, during times of high risk [e.g., on duty at a sports stadium], or just in response to IED events). It is critical that incident commanders base protective equipment and tactical movement guidance at the incident scene on a situational assessment of the IED risk, particularly when IEDs with significant net explosive weight are suspected or confirmed to be present. These types of IEDs, including

---

[xxv] *Blast injuries are the result of the rapid chemical conversion of a solid or liquid into highly pressurized gasses that expand rapidly and compress the surrounding air. This generates a pressure pulse, which spreads as a blast wave in all directions. The effects of the blast wave are more intense in a confined space like a building or bus. The shock wave is amplified as it is reflected off walls, floors, and the ceiling. If the blast occurs outside, the blast wave will dissipate rapidly. It is understood that over-pressure phenomena may enhance the lethality of blast effect for explosions that occur in confined spaces.*

vehicle bombs, may produce blast overpressure effects that would not be mitigated by typical protective equipment or available cover. A false sense of security among first responders could result if net explosive weight is not considered when determining protective equipment or tactical movement guidance to responders.

Protective Equipment Commonly Worn

Most law enforcement officers responding to the incident will be wearing Type II or IIIA bullet resistant vests, designed to stop bullets from most handguns, and shotgun pellets. Given the expected injuries, this level of protective equipment may not provide protection from blast overpressure and fragmentation, and extremities will be vulnerable. First responders other than law enforcement typically do not wear ballistic protective equipment. Civilians at public places will not be wearing any form of ballistic protective equipment.

Protective Equipment Risk Mitigation Considerations

The NIJ body armor standard specifies the ballistic threats that body armor must reliably protect against. This standard does not specify a requirement for ballistic resistant vests to protect against fragmentation threats. The Type II or IIIA ballistic resistant vests that law enforcement officers are most commonly issued will likely not protect against fragmentation and blast overpressure effects from an IED threat. Use of Type IV body armor may increase the probability of protection against fragmentation and blast overpressure. However, further research and development is required to validate the performance of NIJ-approved body armor against fragmentation threats and to provide guidance on what level of protection should be worn to respond to this type of IED event.

Response and Incident Management Considerations

Maximize interoperability through existing MOUs/MOAs/SOPs, as well as through frequent exercises, planning, and training. These efforts will ultimately aid in reducing time from injury to treatment. During response, and while on the scene of the incident, use unified command with a mutual understanding of each responder's role (EMS, fire, and law enforcement). Strive to communicate on common frequencies and use standardized terminology. Ensure all responders (regardless of discipline—EMS, fire, law enforcement) are trained and equipped to provide early, aggressive hemorrhage control; use protective equipment (which includes ballistic vests, helmets, and eyewear); and use integrated response and incident management.

Medical Response System

An IED detonation has the potential of instantly producing hundreds of casualties (there were over 700 casualties after the Oklahoma City bombing) with injuries that range across the entire spectrum of severity. A system-wide medical response to this event should be well-coordinated, incorporating the lessons learned from the military (both system and individual patient care) and experiences from domestic and international bombings. Unlike the management of routine emergencies, the response to IED incidents will be extraordinary for the Nation's trauma and EMS systems.

System-wide efforts should include activities ranging from self-care, buddy-care, and bystander care to proper and effective prehospital triaging and patient transport to get the right patients to the appropriate medical facilities in a swift and orderly manner. The efforts include prehospital emergency medical services, ground ambulances, rotary and fixed wing aircraft patient transport, designated trauma centers, hospitals, and rehabilitation facilities.

Prehospital Emergency Medical Services Considerations

Patient-Based Considerations: The last decade of war has seen significant advances in the ability of prehospital care to impact the mortality of combat wounds. The ability to stop life-threatening bleeding from extremity wounds has been demonstrated to reduce the number of treatable exsanguination deaths.

As IEDs have become a common source of wounding in the wars in Iraq and Afghanistan, and as the use of IEDs in the United States (the Boston Marathon bombing on April 15, 2013) has become a reality, civilian adoption of some military clinical practices that are a significant departure from traditional prehospital care should be considered:

- Aggressive hemorrhage control—including use of tourniquets and, where appropriate, hemostatic agents
- Aggressive airway management, including "sit up and lean forward" airway positioning
- Training all first responders in self-care, buddy care, and bystander care

System-Wide Implications

Experience from bombing attacks occurring in other countries demonstrates common prehospital care system challenges, including multiple simultaneous attacks that cause an enormous number of casualties that exceed the available resources of EMS responders. The adoption of techniques that are suitable for use in self-care, buddy-care, bystander care, and care delivered by first responders is essential to extend the depth of responders available to provide immediate life-saving care.

EMS must rapidly and accurately triage casualties at the incident site and expeditiously transport those identified for "immediate care" into an appropriate hospital setting. It is imperative that pre-hospital triaging of wounded patients be as efficient and accurate as possible. Over-triage of patients over-taxes specialty centers that are designed to care for more significantly injured patients, while under-triaging of patients puts critically wounded patients into facilities that may not be able to provide the life-saving care needed. In addition to proper triage, care must be taken to regulate the transportation of casualties in order to direct victims to the hospital best suited for providing the necessary level of care for the type and severity of injuries they have sustained. Often the closest hospital is quickly overwhelmed by injured transported by ambulances, police cars, and privately owned vehicles, as well as the "walking wounded". Because the influx of patients to the nearest hospital is dictated by human behavior outside control of the system, the EMS system must recognize this likelihood and plan for redistribution of injured patients such that the closest hospital can return to maximum functionality as soon as possible. Incident managers should also anticipate the need to provide for safety and security with the arrival of injured persons' family members, the "psychologically shocked," and the media.

EMS providers must also be cognizant of patients who appear otherwise well (uninjured), but may have traumatic brain injuries, tympanic membrane damage, and/or internal hollow organ damage due to the blast effects of the explosion. These considerations should be reinforced through exercise, planning, protocols, and training.

Hospital-Based Trauma System Considerations

Hospital challenges experienced in foreign and domestic terrorist bombings include:
- Difficulty in acquiring information from the scene
- Maldistribution of patients (e.g., two of 15 hospitals receiving approximately 60 percent of casualties from the scene in one large-scale event)

- A requirement for large numbers of hospital medical personnel to adequately treat the wounded
- The need to implement mass casualty contingency plans at every point of care (e.g., radiology postponing imaging an ankle sprain to rule out a fracture)
- Concern that the hospital may be a target
- Activation of Mass Transfusion Protocols, based on scope of injuries
- Activation of staff augmentation/call back plans, based on scope of injuries
- Initiation of patient movement/transfer plans, based on scope of injuries

Medical leaders of responses to bombings have noted that in many cases the majority of the injured and dead from large events present at the hospital closest to the scene. Patients able to leave the scene may forego EMS triage and present at hospitals before more severely injured patients arrive. The large influx of patients may exceed the hospital's capability to provide care, resulting in a "functional collapse" from inability to meet the demand spike. When this occurs, there is a compelling need to redistribute patients.

Distribution of patients among hospitals, so that no one hospital exceeds its resources, is a key principle in addressing medical surge capacity following bombing attacks that result in a significant number of casualties.

To address the large number of patients arriving at local facilities, local hospitals will need the swift assistance of incoming health care providers to assist with re-triage of the arriving casualties and the provision of appropriate services to patients. This influx will include additional doctors, nurses, medical specialists, such as blood bank technologists and respiratory therapists, mental health providers, and chaplains. In addition, there will likely be the need for law enforcement personnel to maintain order and security. In the hours immediately after the blast, these additional personnel will likely come from surrounding communities and may include health care professionals from beyond the local area. While pre-event planning for cross-town (local) hospital credentialing and privileging of responding health care professionals can be arranged with relative ease, the issue of expeditious out-of-state credentialing and privileging of medical professionals responding to natural or man-made disasters can be more challenging.

Scenario 6: Discovery/Recovery of Homemade Explosives (Not an Attack)

Many who seek explosives try to avoid detection by making their own explosives, often using ingredients and techniques found in on-line instructions. These "homemade" explosives are particularly dangerous, as they are made by inexperienced individuals outside of a formal manufacturing environment and without adequate quality control procedures. The homemade manufacture of primary explosives such as Hexamethlene Triperoxide Diamine (HMTD), Triacetone-Triperoxide (TATP), and Lead Azide are of greatest concern due to their unpredictable nature as well as sensitivity to heat, friction, and shock. First responders including fire/HAZMAT, paramedics, and law enforcement are particularly vulnerable as clandestine labs encountered may look similar to illicit drug labs. In this type of scenario, the victim—either manufacturer or first responder—is often in direct contact with the explosive materials.

EXAMPLE: You are on the scene of a basement fire where firefighters have removed a victim who is unresponsive, but alive. The victim has blast injuries and amputation of his right hand and several fingers from his left hand. The firefighters indicate that the fire is contained, but that there are several containers of unknown materials adjacent to where the fire and reported explosion occurred...

Expected Injury Patterns

For those who survive this event, injuries are often burns and/or traumatic amputation of fingers or limbs, soft tissue injuries, ocular injuries, and ruptured eardrums, depending on the quantity and type of homemade explosive encountered.

Protective Equipment and Barriers

In the absence of further patients requiring care, the scene should be isolated, and only entered by first responders with the appropriate level of protective equipment. A determination will need to be made on scene as to whether flash, hazmat or EOD (bomb suit) protection is indicated. It is critical that incident commanders base protective equipment and tactical movement guidance at the incident scene on a situation assessment of the IED risk, particularly when IEDs with significant net explosive weight are suspected or confirmed to be present. These types of IEDs, including vehicle bombs, may produce overpressure blast effects regardless of fragmentation that would not be mitigated by typical protective equipment or available cover. A false sense of security among first responders could result if net explosive weight is not considered when determining protective equipment or tactical movement guidance to responders.

Protective Equipment Commonly Worn

Law enforcement officers will wear Type II or IIIA bullet resistant vests, designed to stop bullets from most handguns, shotgun pellets, and blunt shrapnel. First responders other than law enforcement typically do not wear ballistic protective equipment. Fire responders wear fire resistant jackets/pants with helmets, which provide thermal protection. Explosive Ordnance Disposal/bomb technicians wear either a full bomb suit or, in some circumstances, less restrictive protective equipment to improve maneuverability.

Response and Incident Management Considerations

Maximize interoperability through existing MOUs/MOAs/SOPs, as well as through frequent exercises, planning, and training. These efforts will ultimately aid in reducing time from injury to treatment. During response, and while on the scene of the incident, use unified command with a mutual understanding of each responder's role (EMS, fire, and law enforcement). Strive to communicate on common frequencies and use standardized terminology. Ensure all responders (regardless of discipline—EMS, fire, law enforcement) are trained and equipped to provide early, aggressive hemorrhage control; use protective equipment (which includes ballistic vests, helmets, and eyewear); and use integrated response and incident management.

Prehospital Emergency Medical Services Considerations

Patient-Based Considerations: The last decade of war has seen significant advances in the ability of prehospital care to impact the mortality of combat wounds. The ability to stop life-threatening bleeding from extremity wounds has been demonstrated to reduce the number of treatable exsanguination deaths.

As IEDs have become a common source of wounding in the wars in Iraq and Afghanistan, and as the use of IEDs in the United States (the Boston Marathon bombing on April 15, 2013) has become a reality, civilian adoption of some military clinical practices that are a significant departure from traditional prehospital care should be considered:

- Aggressive hemorrhage control—including use of tourniquets and, where appropriate, hemostatic agents
- Aggressive airway management, including "sit up and lean forward" airway positioning
- Training all first responders in self-care, buddy care, and bystander care
- In this scenario, the need for decontamination of patients and responders must be considered

Scenario 7: Active Shooter with Access Denial to First Responders

Two shooters attack an indoor public building using firearms, and disperse potentially lethal chemicals in an effort to deny first responder access to the scene. The shooters placed buckets of chemicals adjacent to two primary entry/exit points, creating toxic clouds to block first responders, and then opened fire with semi-automatic weapons, handguns, and shotguns within the center of the building, where approximately 300 people were gathered.

EXAMPLE: You are called to the scene of an indoor shopping mall on a busy day. As the first arriving unit, you see people running from the facility and several victims on the ground immediately outside the exit door in front of you. Several of the people who escaped are in apparent distress and are having trouble breathing. There are three victims who are bleeding and are being cared for by bystanders. You also see a white cloud coming out of the door and hear gunfire from what appears to be several different sources...

Expected Injury Patterns

Multiple gunshot wounds from various caliber weapons; wide-spread casualties from gunshot wounds, chemical exposure, and care delay; and non-firearm-related injuries associated with attempts to escape (lacerations, fractures). The chemicals produce hazardous to potentially lethal effects and a barrier that will significantly delay access by all first responders not prepared to enter into a hazardous materials environment. Traditional HAZ/MAT response results in delays that will promote wide-spread hemorrhage.

Protective Equipment and Barriers

First responders should consider wearing protective equipment to mitigate ballistic, respiratory and mucous membrane, and dermal hazards. Utilizing available barriers or structural walls can also provide protective cover and/or concealment for first responders within the shooter's field of fire. Preventive measures also include use of ballistic protective equipment, although soft body armor and ceramic plate body armor may not protect against fragmentation or blast overpressure effects from IEDs. Most protective equipment is focused on ballistic protection and may have unproven or limited value for mitigating fragmentation or blast overpressure, particularly for devices with larger net explosive weights, such as vehicle bombs. For protective equipment and barriers to be effective, they must be implemented proactively; they are of little use when the explosive event is random and enacted on an unsuspecting, unprotected group of individuals. Ballistic protective equipment will also give some level of protection should an IED attack be combined with an active shooter event. Experience indicates attackers may plan to detonate secondary or subsequent IEDs that target first responders or receiving hospitals.

Protective Equipment Commonly Worn

Most law enforcement officers responding to the incident will be wearing Type II or IIIA bullet resistant vests, designed to stop bullets from most handguns, and shotgun pellets. First responders other than law enforcement typically do not wear ballistic protective equipment. Civilians at public places such will not be wearing any form of ballistic protective equipment.

Protective Equipment Risk Mitigation Considerations

Responders should utilize the highest level of protective equipment available to them—ideally Type IV ballistic vests and helmets when responding to active shooter incidents. The NIJ body armor standard specifies ballistic threats that body armor must reliably protect against.[44][45]

Protection against common industrial hazardous chemicals—with a focus on respiratory, eyes, mucous membranes and skin protection—can be provided by first responder turnout gear, SCBA (Self-Contained Breathing Apparatus), gas masks, and Victim Rescue Units or Tyvek® suits.

Response and Incident Management Considerations

Maximize interoperability through existing MOUs/MOAs/SOPs, as well as through frequent exercises, planning, and training. These efforts will ultimately aid in reducing time from injury to treatment. During response, and while on the scene of the incident, use unified command with a mutual understanding of each responder's role (EMS, fire, and law enforcement). Strive to communicate on common frequencies and use standardized terminology. Ensure all responders (regardless of discipline—EMS, fire, law enforcement) are trained and equipped to provide early, aggressive hemorrhage control; use protective equipment (which includes ballistic vests, helmets, and eyewear); and use integrated response and incident management.

Medical Response System

An active shooter incident complicated by a hazardous materials release has the potential to produce large numbers of casualties with injuries that range across the entire spectrum of severity. In addition to mass casualty trauma care, high consideration of decontamination requirements must be taken. A system-wide medical response to this event should be well-coordinated, incorporating the lessons learned from the military (both system and individual patient care) and experiences from domestic and international incidents. Unlike the management of routine emergencies, the response to active shooter incidents will be extraordinary for the Nation's trauma and EMS systems.

System-wide efforts should include activities ranging from self-care, buddy-care, and bystander care to proper and effective prehospital triaging and patient transport to get the right patients to the appropriate medical facilities in a swift and orderly manner. The efforts include prehospital emergency medical services, ground ambulances, rotary and fixed wing aircraft patient transport, designated trauma centers, hospitals, and rehabilitation facilities.

Prehospital Emergency Medical Services Considerations

Patient-Based Considerations: The last decade of war has seen significant advances in the ability of prehospital care to impact the mortality of combat wounds. The ability to stop life-threatening bleeding from extremity wounds has been demonstrated to reduce the number of treatable exsanguination deaths.

As active shooter incidents have become a common source of wounding in the United States, civilian adoption of some military clinical practices that are a significant departure from traditional prehospital care should be considered:

- Aggressive hemorrhage control—including use of tourniquets and, where appropriate, hemostatic agents
- Aggressive airway management, including "sit up and lean forward" airway positioning
- Training all first responders in self-care, buddy care, and bystander care
- In this scenario, the need for decontamination of patients and responders must be considered

System-Wide Implications

Experience from attacks (active shooter incidents) occurring in other countries demonstrates common prehospital care system challenges, including multiple simultaneous attacks that cause an enormous number of casualties that exceed the available resources of EMS responders. The adoption of techniques that are suitable for use in self-care, buddy-care, bystander care, and care delivered by first responders is essential to extend the depth of responders available to provide immediate life-saving care.

EMS must rapidly and accurately triage casualties at the incident site and expeditiously transport those identified for "immediate care" into an appropriate hospital setting. It is imperative that pre-hospital triaging of wounded patients be as efficient and accurate as possible. Over-triage of patients over-taxes specialty centers that are designed to care for more significantly injured patients, while under-triaging of patients puts critically wounded patients into facilities that may not be able to provide the life-saving care needed. In addition to proper triage, care must be taken to regulate the transportation of casualties in order to direct victims to the hospital best suited for providing the necessary level of care for the type and severity of injuries they have sustained. Often the closest hospital is quickly overwhelmed by injured transported by ambulances, police cars, and privately owned vehicles, as well as the "walking wounded". Because the influx of patients to the nearest hospital is dictated by human behavior outside control of the system, the EMS system must recognize this likelihood and plan for redistribution of injured patients such that the closest hospital can return to maximum functionality as soon as possible. Incident managers should also anticipate the need to provide for safety and security with the arrival of injured persons' family members, the "psychologically shocked," and the media.

From a law enforcement perspective, the following should be considered:

- Law enforcement units should be trained in active shooter response, to include deployment of a contact team and a follow-on rescue team, depending on local resources and system configuration.

- All first responders (EMS, fire, and law enforcement) should be trained and practiced to work together in active shooter scenarios.

- Active shooter first response should focus on traditional Care Under Fire injuries with immediate "Extraction" from the site of the attack as a priority. All casualties should be directed or moved to a "Safe Point" (a secure location near the attack) by extraction teams where the casualties will be re-triaged and treated for transfer.

- Interoperability between EMS, fire and law enforcement personnel must be exercised and an understanding of the responsibilities and actions of all parties is essential. This is achieved through mutual trainings, well-developed policies, and tabletop exercises.

- State and local officials should promote CERTs to deliver civilian training in conjunction with non-governmental organizations.

Experience from active shooter incidents and bombing attacks demonstrates common prehospital care system challenges, including multiple simultaneous attacks that cause an enormous number of casualties that exceed the available resources of EMS responders. The adoption of techniques that are suitable for use in self-care, buddy-care, bystander care, and care delivered by first responders is essential to extend the range of persons providing immediate life-saving care. First responders should develop plans for working on "contaminated casualties".

EMS providers must also be cognizant of patients who appear otherwise well (uninjured), but may have hidden injuries and exposure to hazardous materials. These considerations should be reinforced through exercise, planning, protocols, and training.

Hospital-Based Trauma System Considerations

Hospital challenges experienced in foreign and domestic active shooter incidents include:

- Difficulty in acquiring information from the scene
- Maldistribution of patients (e.g., two of 15 hospitals receiving approximately 60 percent of casualties from the scene in one large-scale event)
- A requirement for large numbers of hospital medical personnel to adequately treat the wounded
- The need to implement mass casualty contingency plans at every point of care (e.g., radiology postponing imaging an ankle sprain to rule out a fracture)
- Concern that the hospital may be a target
- Activation of Mass Transfusion Protocols, based on scope of injuries
- Activation of staff augmentation/call back plans, based on scope of injuries
- Initiation of patient movement/transfer plans, based on scope of injuries

Medical leaders of responses to attacks have noted that in many cases the majority of the injured and dead from large events present at the hospital closest to the scene. Patients able to leave the scene may forego EMS triage and present at hospitals before more severely injured patients arrive. The large influx of patients may exceed the hospital's capability to provide care, resulting in a "functional collapse" from inability to meet the demand spike. When this occurs, there is a compelling need to redistribute patients.

Distribution of patients among hospitals, so that no one hospital exceeds its resources, is a key principle in addressing medical surge capacity following bombing attacks that result in a significant number of casualties.

To address the large number of patients arriving at local facilities, local hospitals will need the swift assistance of incoming health care providers to assist with re-triage of the arriving casualties and the provision of appropriate services to patients. This influx will include additional doctors, nurses, medical specialists, such as blood bank technologists and respiratory therapists, mental health providers, and chaplains. In addition, there will likely be the need for law enforcement personnel to maintain order and security. In the hours immediately after the in-cident, these additional personnel will likely come from surrounding communities and may include health care professionals from beyond the local area. While pre-event planning for cross-town (local) hospital credentialing and privileging of responding health care professionals can be arranged with relative ease, the issue of expedi-tious out-of-state credentialing and privileging of medical professionals responding to natural or man-made disasters can be more challenging.

Patient Movement/Transfer Considerations

As the patient load builds at local hospitals, some of the critically injured patients should be moved to other medical care facilities to optimize patient care. This will include movement to Level-1 trauma centers and other hospitals to better balance inpatient bed, operating room, intensive care unit, and rehabilitation bed utilization. Depending on the locality of the incident, this may include moving patients to other communities or across state lines. Long-distance transport of acutely injured patients will likely require aeromedical evacuation capabilities.

Scenario 8: Active Shooter in a Public Commercial Facility

A lone gunman enters a public commercial facility and starts methodically moving through the building, shooting everyone he encounters. The gunman is armed with two handguns, a shotgun and a semi-automatic rifle. According to a witness who escaped, there are approximately 60 individuals in the facility. The gunmen used bike locks to immobilize exit doors.

EXAMPLE: You are the first arriving unit to a supermarket where terrified people are running from side doors and are seeking cover in the parking lot and surrounding area. You see four people with obvious gunshot wounds, one of whom is obviously deceased. You hear continued gunfire from your location…

Expected Injury Patterns

Multiple gunshot wounds from various caliber weapons, wide-spread casualties from gunshot wounds and care delay, and non-firearm-related injuries associated with attempts to escape (lacerations, fractures).

Protective Equipment and Barriers

First responders should consider wearing some level of ballistic protective equipment. Utilizing available barriers or structural walls can also provide protective cover and/or concealment for first responders within the shooter's field of fire. Preventive measures also include use of ballistic protective equipment, although soft body armor and ceramic plate body armor may not protect against fragmentation or blast overpressure effects from IEDs. Most protective equipment is focused on ballistic protection and may have unproven or limited value for mitigating fragmentation or blast overpressure, particularly for devices with larger net explosive weights, such as vehicle bombs. For protective equipment and barriers to be effective, they must be implemented proactively; they are of little use when the explosive event is random and enacted on an unsuspecting, unprotected group of individuals. Ballistic protective equipment will also give some level of protection should an IED attack be combined with an active shooter event. Experience indicates attackers may plan to detonate secondary or subsequent IEDs that target first responders or receiving hospitals.

Protective Equipment Commonly Worn

Most law enforcement officers responding to the incident will be wearing Type II or IIIA bullet resistant vests, designed to stop bullets from most handguns, and shotgun pellets. First responders other than law enforcement typically do not wear ballistic protective equipment. Civilians at public places such will not be wearing any form of ballistic protective equipment.

Protective Equipment Risk Mitigation Considerations

Responders should utilize the highest level of protective equipment available to them—ideally Type IV ballistic vests and helmets when responding to active shooter incidents. The NIJ body armor standard specifies ballistic threats that body armor must reliably protect against.[44][45]

Response and Incident Management Considerations

Maximize interoperability through existing MOUs/MOAs/SOPs, as well as through frequent exercises, planning, and training. These efforts will ultimately aid in reducing time from injury to treatment. During response, and while on the scene of the incident, use unified command with a mutual understanding of each responder's role (EMS, fire, and law enforcement). Strive to communicate on common frequencies and use standardized terminology. Ensure all responders (regardless of discipline—EMS, fire, law enforcement) are trained and equipped to provide early, aggressive hemorrhage control; use protective equipment (which includes ballistic vests, helmets, and eyewear); and use integrated response and incident management.

Medical Response System

A system-wide medical response to this event should be well-coordinated, incorporating the lessons learned from the military (both system and individual patient care) and experiences from domestic and international active shooter incidents. Unlike the management of routine emergencies, the response to active shooter incidents will be extraordinary for the Nation's trauma and EMS systems.

System-wide efforts should include activities ranging from self-care, buddy-care, and bystander care to proper and effective prehospital triaging and patient transport to get the right patients to the appropriate medical facilities in a swift and orderly manner. The efforts include prehospital emergency medical services, ground ambulances, rotary and fixed wing aircraft patient transport, designated trauma centers, hospitals, and rehabilitation facilities.

Prehospital Emergency Medical Services Considerations

Patient-Based Considerations: The last decade of war has seen significant advances in the ability of prehospital care to impact the mortality of combat wounds. The ability to stop life-threatening bleeding from extremity wounds has been demonstrated to reduce the number of treatable exsanguination deaths.

As active shooter incidents have become a common source of wounding in the United States, civilian adoption of some military clinical practices that are a significant departure from traditional prehospital care should be considered:

- Aggressive hemorrhage control—including use of tourniquets and, where appropriate, hemostatic agents
- Aggressive airway management, including "sit up and lean forward" airway positioning
- Training all first responders in self-care, buddy care, and bystander care

System-Wide Implications

Experience from terrorist attacks (active shooter incidents) occurring in other countries demonstrates common prehospital care system challenges, including multiple simultaneous attacks that cause an enormous number of casualties that exceed the available resources of EMS responders. The adoption of techniques that are suitable for use in self-care, buddy-care, bystander care, and care delivered by first responders is essential to extend the depth of responders available to provide immediate life-saving care.

EMS must rapidly and accurately triage casualties at the incident site and expeditiously transport those identified for "immediate care" into an appropriate hospital setting. It is imperative that pre-hospital triaging of wounded patients be as efficient and accurate as possible. Over-triage of patients over-taxes specialty centers that are designed to care for more significantly injured patients, while under-triaging of patients puts critically wounded patients into facilities that may not be able to provide the life-saving care needed. In addition to proper triage, care must be taken to regulate the transportation of casualties in order to direct victims to the hospital best suited for providing the necessary level of care for the type and severity of injuries they have sustained. Often the closest hospital is quickly overwhelmed by injured transported by ambulances, police cars, and privately owned vehicles, as well as the "walking wounded". Because the influx of patients to the nearest hospital is dictated by human behavior outside control of the system, the EMS system must recognize this likelihood and plan for redistribution of injured patients such that the closest hospital can return to maximum functionality as soon as possible. Incident managers should also anticipate the need to provide for safety and security with the arrival of injured persons' family members, the "psychologically shocked," and the media.

From a law enforcement perspective, the following should be considered:

- Law enforcement units should be trained in active shooter response, to include deployment of a contact team and a follow-on rescue team, depending on local resources and system configuration.

- All first responders (EMS, fire, and law enforcement) should be trained and practiced to work together in active shooter scenarios.

- Active shooter first response should focus on traditional Care Under Fire injuries with immediate "Extraction" from the site of the attack as a priority. All casualties should be directed or moved to a "Safe Point" (a secure location near the attack) by extraction teams where the casualties will be re-triaged and treated for transfer.

- Interoperability between EMS, fire and law enforcement personnel must be exercised, and an understanding of the responsibilities and actions of all parties is essential. This is achieved through mutual trainings, well-developed policies, and tabletop exercises.

- State and local officials should promote CERTs to deliver civilian training in conjunction with non-governmental organizations.

Experience from active shooter incidents and bombing attacks demonstrates common prehospital care system challenges, including multiple simultaneous attacks that cause an enormous number of casualties that exceed the available resources of EMS responders. The adoption of techniques that are suitable for use in self-care, buddy-care, bystander care, and care delivered by first responders is essential to extend the range of persons providing immediate life-saving care.

Hospital-Based Trauma System Considerations

Hospital challenges experienced in foreign and domestic active shooter incidents include:

- Difficulty in acquiring information from the scene

- Maldistribution of patients (e.g., two of 15 hospitals receiving approximately 60 percent of casualties from the scene in one large-scale event)

- A requirement for large numbers of hospital medical personnel to adequately treat the wounded

- The need to implement mass casualty contingency plans at every point of care (e.g., radiology postponing imaging an ankle sprain to rule out a fracture)

- Concern that the hospital may be a target

- Activation of Mass Transfusion Protocols, based on scope of injuries

- Activation of staff augmentation/call back plans, based on scope of injuries

- Initiation of patient movement/transfer plans, based on scope of injuries

Medical leaders of responses to attacks have noted that in many cases the majority of the injured and dead from large events present at the hospital closest to the scene. Patients able to leave the scene may forego EMS triage and present at hospitals before more severely injured patients arrive. The large influx of patients may exceed the hospital's capability to provide care, resulting in a "functional collapse" from inability to meet the demand spike. When this occurs, there is a compelling need to redistribute patients.

Distribution of patients among hospitals, so that no one hospital exceeds its resources, is a key principle in addressing medical surge capacity following bombing attacks that result in a significant number of casualties.

To address the large number of patients arriving at local facilities, local hospitals will need the swift assistance of incoming health care providers to assist with re-triage of the arriving casualties and the provision of appropriate services to patients. This influx will include additional doctors, nurses, medical specialists, such as blood bank technologists and respiratory therapists, mental health providers, and chaplains. In addition, there will likely be the need for law enforcement personnel to maintain order and security. In the hours immediately after the blast, these additional personnel will likely come from surrounding communities and may include health care professionals from beyond the local area. While pre-event planning for cross-town (local) hospital credentialing and privileging of responding health care professionals can be arranged with relative ease, the issue of expeditious out-of-state credentialing and privileging of medical professionals responding to natural or man-made disasters can be more challenging.

Patient Movement/Transfer Considerations

As the patient load builds at local hospitals, some of the critically injured patients should be moved to other medical care facilities to optimize patient care. This will include movement to Level-1 trauma centers and other hospitals to better balance inpatient bed, operating room, intensive care unit, and rehabilitation bed utilization. Depending on the locality of the incident, this may include moving patients to other communities or across state lines. Long-distance transport of acutely injured patients will likely require aeromedical evacuation capabilities.

Distribution of patients among hospitals, so that no one hospital exceeds its resources, is a key principle in addressing medical surge capacity following bombing attacks that result in a significant number of casualties.

To address the large number of patients arriving at local facilities, local hospitals will need the swift assistance of incoming health care providers to assist with re-triage of the arriving casualties and the provision of appropriate services to patients. This influx will include additional doctors, nurses, medical specialists, such as blood bank technologists and respiratory therapists, mental health providers, and chaplains. In addition, there will likely be the need for law enforcement personnel to maintain order and security. In the hours immediately after the incident, these additional personnel will likely come from surrounding communities and may include health care professionals from beyond the local area. While pre-event planning for cross-town (local) hospital credentialing and privileging of responding health care professionals can be arranged with relative ease, the issue of expeditious out-of-state credentialing and privileging of medical professionals responding to natural or man-made disasters can be more challenging.

Scenario 9: Active Shooter in an Open, Outdoor, Unbounded Location

A single gunman enters a building and takes and elevated position, overlooking a crowded courtyard. The gunman is armed with handguns and a scoped hunting rifle. There are approximately 165 people currently in the courtyard as the gunman commences firing into the crowd.

EXAMPLE: You are the first arriving unit to a reported active shooter incident at an open courtyard at an academic institution. As you approach, there are many people running away from the facility. You notice several injured people with bystanders rendering care, as well as several victims who are obviously deceased. The crowd egressing is panic-stricken and seeking cover as you hear continued gunfire.

Expected Injury Patterns

Multiple gunshot wounds from mostly high-caliber weapons, wide-spread casualties from gunshot wounds and care delay, and non-firearm-related injuries associated with attempts to escape (lacerations, fractures).

Protective Equipment and Barriers

First responders should consider wearing protective equipment to mitigate ballistic, respiratory and mucous membrane, and dermal hazards. Utilizing available barriers or structural walls can also provide protective cover and/or concealment for first responders within the shooter's field of fire. Ballistic protective equipment includes soft body armor and ceramic plate body armor, and may also provide some level of protection should the active shooter event be combined with a secondary or subsequent IED attack. Experience indicates attackers may plan to detonate secondary or subsequent IEDs that target first responders or receiving hospitals.

Considerations for first responder ballistic protective equipment should include what type of equipment is best suited for EMS responders and when it should be worn (every shift, during times of high risk [e.g., on duty at a sports stadium], or just in response to IED events).

Protective Equipment Commonly Worn

Most law enforcement officers responding to the incident will be wearing Type II or IIIA bullet resistant vests, designed to stop bullets from most handguns, and shotgun pellets. First responders other than law enforcement typically do not wear ballistic protective equipment. Civilians at public places such will not be wearing any form of ballistic protective equipment.

Protective Equipment Risk Mitigation Considerations

Responders should utilize the highest level of protective equipment available to them—ideally Type IV ballistic vests and helmets. The NIJ body armor standard specifies ballistic threats that body armor must reliably protect against.[44][45]

Response and Incident Management Considerations

Maximize interoperability to the extent possible (through prior MOUs/MOAs/SOPs) to reduce time from injury to treatment. Strive to communicate on common frequencies and use standardized terminology. Ensure all responders (regardless of discipline—EMS, fire, law enforcement) are trained and equipped to provide early, aggressive hemorrhage control; use body armor; use a more integrated response and incident management.

Flexibility is key in how effectively aid is delivered to the injured—a single solution may not work best in all scenarios (e.g., law enforcement brings the injured out to safety, law enforcement escorts EMS/fire into transitional zones, law enforcement provides care).

Medical Response System

System-wide efforts should include activities ranging from self-care, buddy-care, and bystander care to regional and multi-state trauma responses. The efforts include prehospital emergency medical services, ground ambulances, rotary and fixed wing aircraft patient transport, designated trauma centers, hospitals, and rehabilitation facilities. Unlike the management of routine emergencies, the response to active shooter incidents will be extraordinary for the Nation's trauma and EMS systems.

Prehospital Emergency Medical Services Considerations

Patient-Based Considerations: The last decade of war has seen significant advances in the ability of prehospital care to impact the mortality of combat wounds. The ability to stop life-threatening bleeding from extremity wounds has been demonstrated to reduce the number of treatable exsanguination deaths. Civilian adoption of some military clinical practices that are a significant departure from traditional prehospital care is appropriate:

- Aggressive hemorrhage control—including use of tourniquets and, where appropriate, hemostatic agents
- Aggressive airway management, including "sit up and lean forward" airway positioning
- Training all first responders in self-care, buddy care, and bystander care

System-Wide Implications

Experience from terrorist attacks (active shooter incidents) occurring in other countries demonstrates common prehospital care system challenges, including multiple simultaneous attacks that cause an enormous number of casualties that exceed the available resources of EMS responders. The adoption of techniques that are suitable for use in self-care, buddy-care, bystander care, and care delivered by first responders is essential to extend the depth of responders available to provide immediate life-saving care.

EMS must rapidly and accurately triage casualties at the incident site and expeditiously transport those identified for "immediate care" into an appropriate hospital setting. It is imperative that pre-hospital triaging of wounded patients be as efficient and accurate as possible. Over-triage of patients over-taxes specialty centers that are designed to care for more significantly injured patients, while under-triaging of patients puts critically wounded patients into facilities that may not be able to provide the life-saving care needed. In addition to proper triage, care must be taken to regulate the transportation of casualties in order to direct victims to the hospital best suited for providing the necessary level of care for the type and severity of injuries they have sustained. Often the closest hospital is quickly overwhelmed by injured transported by ambulances, police cars, and privately owned vehicles, as well as the "walking wounded". Because the influx of patients to the nearest hospital is dictated by human behavior outside control of the system, the EMS system must recognize this likelihood and plan for redistribution of injured patients such that the closest hospital can return to maximum functionality as soon as possible. Incident managers should also anticipate the need to provide for safety and security with the arrival of injured persons' family members, the "psychologically shocked," and the media.

From a law enforcement perspective, the following should be considered:

- Law enforcement units should be trained in active shooter response, to include deployment of a contact team and a follow-on rescue team, depending on local resources and system configuration.

- All first responders (EMS, fire, and law enforcement) should be trained and practiced to work together in active shooter scenarios.

- Active shooter first response should focus on traditional Care Under Fire injuries with immediate "Extraction" from the site of the attack as a priority. All casualties should be directed or moved to a "Safe Point" (a secure location near the attack) by extraction teams where the casualties will be re-triaged and treated for transfer.

- Interoperability between EMS, fire, and law enforcement personnel must be exercised, and an understanding of the responsibilities and actions of all parties is essential. This is achieved through mutual trainings, well-developed policies, and tabletop exercises.

State and local officials should promote CERTs to deliver civilian training in conjunction with non-governmental organizations.

Hospital-Based Trauma System Considerations

Hospital challenges experienced in foreign and domestic active shooter incidents include:

- Difficulty in acquiring information from the scene

- Maldistribution of patients (e.g., two of 15 hospitals receiving approximately 60 percent of casualties from the scene in one large-scale event)

- A requirement for large numbers of hospital medical personnel to adequately treat the wounded

- The need to implement mass casualty contingency plans at every point of care (e.g., radiology postponing imaging an ankle sprain to rule out a fracture)

- Concern that the hospital may be a target

- Activation of Mass Transfusion Protocols, based on scope of injuries

- Activation of staff augmentation/call back plans, based on scope of injuries

- Initiation of patient movement/transfer plans, based on scope of injuries

Medical leaders of responses to attacks have noted that in many cases the majority of the injured and dead from large events present at the hospital closest to the scene. Patients able to leave the scene may forego EMS triage and present at hospitals before more severely injured patients arrive. The large influx of patients may exceed the hospital's capability to provide care, resulting in a "functional collapse" from inability to meet the demand spike. When this occurs, there is a compelling need to redistribute patients.

Distribution of patients among hospitals, so that no one hospital exceeds its resources, is a key principle in addressing medical surge capacity following bombing attacks that result in a significant number of casualties.

To address the large number of patients arriving at local facilities, local hospitals will need the swift assistance of incoming health care providers to assist with re-triage of the arriving casualties and the provision of appropriate services to patients. This influx will include additional doctors, nurses, medical specialists, such as blood bank technologists and respiratory therapists, mental health providers, and chaplains. In addition, there will likely be the need for law enforcement personnel to maintain order and security. In the hours immediately after the blast, these additional personnel will likely come from surrounding communities and may include health care professionals from beyond the local area. While pre-event planning for cross-town (local) hospital credentialing and privileging of responding health care professionals can be arranged with relative ease, the issue of expeditious out-of-state credentialing and privileging of medical professionals responding to natural or man-made disasters can be more challenging.

Patient Movement/Transfer Considerations

As the patient load builds at local hospitals, some of the critically injured patients should be moved to other medical care facilities to optimize patient care. This will include movement to Level-1 trauma centers and other hospitals to better balance inpatient bed, operating room, intensive care unit, and rehabilitation bed utilization. Depending on the locality of the incident, this may include moving patients to other communities or across state lines. Long-distance transport of acutely injured patients will likely require aeromedical evacuation capabilities.

Scenario 10: Active Shooter in a Public Sports Complex

Three gunmen enter a sporting complex that is filled with spectators. One gunman is located at an exit gate and the other two are positioned in the stadium and they all commence firing randomly at spectators. They are armed with handguns, shotguns and semi-automatic rifles. The facility currently has approximately 24,000 people in attendance.

EXAMPLE: You are the first arriving unit to a reported active shooter incident at a sport complex. As you approach, there are many people running away from the facility. Several security personnel and law enforcement officers working the event are seen on the outside perimeter of the complex...

Expected Injury Patterns

Multiple victims with gunshot wounds from various caliber weapons, wide-spread casualties from gunshot wounds and care delay, and non-firearm-related injuries associated with attempts to escape (lacerations, fractures).

Protective Equipment and Barriers

First responders should consider wearing protective equipment to mitigate ballistic, respiratory and mucous membrane, and dermal hazards. Utilizing available barriers or structural walls can also provide protective cover and/or concealment for first responders within the shooter's field of fire. Ballistic protective equipment includes soft body armor and ceramic plate body armor, and may also provide some level of protection should the active shooter event be combined with a secondary or subsequent IED attack. Experience indicates attackers may plan to detonate secondary or subsequent IEDs that target first responders or receiving hospitals.

Considerations for first responder ballistic protective equipment should include what type of equipment is best suited for EMS responders and when it should be worn (every shift, during times of high risk [e.g., on duty at a sports stadium], or just in response to IED events).

Protective Equipment Commonly Worn

Most law enforcement officers responding to the incident will be wearing Type II or IIIA bullet resistant vests, designed to stop bullets from most handguns, and shotgun pellets. First responders other than law enforcement typically do not wear ballistic protective equipment. Civilians at public places such will not be wearing any form of ballistic protective equipment.

Protective Equipment Risk Mitigation Considerations

Responders should utilize the highest level of protective equipment available to them—ideally Type IV ballistic vests and helmets. The NIJ body armor standard specifies ballistic threats that body armor must reliably protect against.[44] [45]

Response and Incident Management Considerations

Maximize interoperability to the extent possible (through prior MOUs/MOAs/SOPs) to reduce time from injury to treatment. Strive to communicate on common frequencies and use standardized terminology. Ensure all responders (regardless of discipline—EMS, fire, law enforcement) are trained and equipped to provide early, aggressive hemorrhage control; use body armor; and use more integrated response and incident management. Flexibility is key in how effectively aid is delivered to the injured—a single solution may not work best in all scenarios (i.e., law enforcement brings the injured out to safety, law enforcement escorts EMS/fire into transitional zones, law enforcement provides care).

Medical Response System

System-wide efforts should include activities ranging from self-care, buddy-care, and bystander care to regional and multi-state trauma responses. The efforts include prehospital emergency medical services, ground ambulances, rotary and fixed wing aircraft patient transport, designated trauma centers, hospitals, and rehabilitation facilities. Unlike the management of routine emergencies, the response to active shooter incidents will be extraordinary for the Nation's trauma and EMS systems.

Prehospital Emergency Medical Services Considerations

Patient-Based Considerations: The last decade of war has seen significant advances in the ability of prehospital care to impact the mortality of combat wounds. The ability to stop life-threatening bleeding from extremity wounds has been demonstrated to reduce the number of treatable exsanguination deaths. Civilian adoption of some military clinical practices that are a significant departure from traditional prehospital care is appropriate:

- Aggressive hemorrhage control—including use of tourniquets and, where appropriate, hemostatic agents
- Aggressive airway management, including "sit up and lean forward" airway positioning
- Training all first responders in self-care, buddy care, and bystander care

System-Wide Implications

Experience from terrorist attacks (active shooter incidents) occurring in other countries demonstrates common prehospital care system challenges, including multiple simultaneous attacks that cause an enormous number of casualties that exceed the available resources of EMS responders. The adoption of techniques that are suitable for use in self-care, buddy-care, bystander care, and care delivered by first responders is essential to extend the depth of responders available to provide immediate life-saving care.

EMS must rapidly and accurately triage casualties at the incident site and expeditiously transport those identified for "immediate care" into an appropriate hospital setting. It is imperative that pre-hospital triaging of wounded patients be as efficient and accurate as possible. Over-triage of patients over-taxes specialty centers that are designed to care for more significantly injured patients, while under-triaging of patients puts critically wounded patients into facilities that may not be able to provide the life-saving care needed. In addition to proper triage, care must be taken to regulate the transportation of casualties in order to direct victims to the hospital best suited for providing the necessary level of care for the type and severity of injuries they have sustained. Often the closest hospital is quickly overwhelmed by injured transported by ambulances, police cars, and privately owned vehicles, as well as the "walking wounded". Because the influx of patients to the nearest hospital is dictated by human behavior outside control of the system, the EMS system must recognize this likelihood and plan for redistribution of injured patients such that the closest hospital can return to maximum functionality as soon as possible. Incident managers should also anticipate the need to provide for safety and security with the arrival of injured persons' family members, the "psychologically shocked," and the media.

From a law enforcement perspective, the following should be considered:

- Law enforcement units should be trained in active shooter response, to include deployment of a contact team and a follow-on rescue team, depending on local resources and system configuration.

- All first responders (EMS, fire, and law enforcement) should be trained and practiced to work together in active shooter scenarios.

- Active shooter first response should focus on traditional Care Under Fire injuries with immediate "Extraction" from the site of the attack as a priority. All casualties should be directed or moved to a "Safe Point" (a secure location near the attack) by extraction teams where the casualties will be re-triaged and treated for transfer.

- Interoperability between EMS, fire, and law enforcement personnel must be exercised, and an understanding of the responsibilities and actions of all parties is essential. This is achieved through mutual trainings, well-developed policies, and tabletop exercises.

- State and local officials should promote CERTs to deliver civilian training in conjunction with non-governmental organizations.

Hospital-Based Trauma System Considerations

Hospital challenges experienced in foreign and domestic active shooter incidents include:

- Difficulty in acquiring information from the scene
- Maldistribution of patients (e.g., two of 15 hospitals receiving approximately 60 percent of casualties from the scene in one large-scale event)
- A requirement for large numbers of hospital medical personnel to adequately treat the wounded
- The need to implement mass casualty contingency plans at every point of care (e.g., radiology postponing imaging an ankle sprain to rule out a fracture)
- Concern that the hospital may be a target
- Activation of Mass Transfusion Protocols, based on scope of injuries
- Activation of staff augmentation/call back plans, based on scope of injuries
- Initiation of patient movement/transfer plans, based on scope of injuries

Medical leaders of responses to attacks have noted that in many cases the majority of the injured and dead from large events present at the hospital closest to the scene. Patients able to leave the scene may forego EMS triage and present at hospitals before more severely injured patients arrive. The large influx of patients may exceed the hospital's capability to provide care, resulting in a "functional collapse" from inability to meet the demand spike. When this occurs, there is a compelling need to redistribute patients.

Distribution of patients among hospitals, so that no one hospital exceeds its resources, is a key principle in addressing medical surge capacity following bombing attacks that result in a significant number of casualties.

To address the large number of patients arriving at local facilities, local hospitals will need the swift assistance of incoming health care providers to assist with re-triage of the arriving casualties and the provision of appropriate services to patients. This influx will include additional doctors, nurses, medical specialists, such as blood bank technologists and respiratory therapists, mental health providers, and chaplains. In addition, there will likely be the need for law enforcement personnel to maintain order and security. In the hours immediately after the blast, these additional personnel will likely come from surrounding communities and may include health care professionals from beyond the local area. While pre-event planning for cross-town (local) hospital credentialing and privileging of responding health care professionals can be arranged with relative ease, the issue of expeditious out-of-state credentialing and privileging of medical professionals responding to natural or man-made disasters can be more challenging.

Patient Movement/Transfer Considerations

As the patient load builds at local hospitals, some of the critically injured patients should be moved to other medical care facilities to optimize patient care. This will include movement to Level-1 trauma centers and other hospitals to better balance inpatient bed, operating room, intensive care unit, and rehabilitation bed utilization. Depending on the locality of the incident, this may include moving patients to other communities or across state lines. Long-distance transport of acutely injured patients will likely require aeromedical evacuation capabilities.

Acronyms Used in this Document

ALS	Advanced Life Support
AP	Armor Piercing
ATEC	U.S. Army Test and Evaluation Command
C-TECC	Committee for Tactical Emergency Casualty Care
CDC	Centers for Disease Control and Prevention
CERT	Community Emergency Response Team
DCR	Damage Control Resuscitation
DoD	Department of Defense
EMS	Emergency Medical Services
EOD	Explosive Ordnance Disposal
FEMA	Federal Emergency Management Agency
FMJ	Full Metal Jacket
IED	Improvised Explosive Device
LE	Law Enforcement
MRC	Medical Reserve Corps
MOA	Memorandum of Agreement
MOU	Memorandum of Understanding
NIJ	National Institute of Justice
NIMS	National Incident Management System
NRF	National Response Framework
NTOA	National Tactical Officers Association
PSAP	Public Safety Answering/Access Points (9-1-1 dispatch centers)
RTF	Rescue Task Force
SCBA	Self-Contained Breathing Apparatus
SOP	Standard Operating Procedure
TBI	Traumatic Brain Injury
TCCC	Tactical Combat Casualty Care
TECC	Tactical Emergency Casualty Care
TIIDE	Terrorism Injuries: Information, Dissemination, and Exchange Project
TTP	Tactics, Techniques, and Procedures
USFA	U.S. Fire Administration
VBID	Vehicle-Borne Improvised Explosive Device

Background Documents (key sources highlighted in bold)

1. Schmidt PJ. Blood and disaster-supply and demand. *N Engl J Med* 2002; 346(8):617.

2. Raja AS, Propper BW, Vandenberg SL, Matchette MW, Rasmussen TE, Johannigman JA, Davidson SB. Imaging utilization during explosive multiple casualty incidents. *J Trauma* 2010; 68:1421-4.

3. Kanter Robert, Moran John. Hospital emergency surge capacity: an empiric New York statewide study. *Ann Emerg Med* 2007; 50(3):314-9.

4. In a moment's notice: surge capacity for terrorist bombings. Challenges and proposed solutions. Centers for Disease Control, 2007. http://emergency.cdc.gov/masscasualties/surgeca-pacity.asp. Accessed November 20, 2008.

5. Greeraedts LM Jr, Demiral H, Schaap NT, et al. Blind transfusion of blood products in exsanguinating trauma patients. *Resuscitation* 2007; 73(3):382-8.

6. Malone DL, Hess JR, Fingerhut A. Massive transfusion practices around the globe and a suggestion for a common massive transfusion protocol. *J Trauma* 2006; 60(6Supplement): S91-6.

7. Phillips TF, Soulier G, Wilson RF. Outcome of massive transfusion exceeding two blood volumes in trauma and emergency surgery. *J Trauma* 1987; 27(8):903-10.

8. Wudel JH, Morris JA Jr, Yates K, Wilson A, Bass SM. Massive transfusion: outcome in blunt trauma patients. *J Trauma* 1991; 31(1):1-7.

9. Scalea TM, Bochicchio KM, Lumpkins K, et al. Early aggressive use of fresh frozen plasma does not improve outcomes in critically injured trauma patients. *Ann Surg* 2008; 248:578-584.

10. Kaji AH, Lewis RJ. Hospital disaster preparedness in Los Angeles County. *Acad Emerg Med* 2006; 13(11):1198-203.

11. Kotwal RS, Montgomery HR, Kotwal BM, et al. Eliminating preventable death on the battlefield. *Arch Surg.* 2011 Dec; 146(12):1350-1358.

12. **Mamczak CN, Elster EA. Complex dismounted IED blast injuries: the initial management of bilateral lower extremity amputations with and without pelvic and perineal involvement. *J Surg Orthop Adv.* 2012 Spring; 21(1):8-14.**

13. **Alfieri KA, Elster EA, Dunne J. Resuscitation and blood utilization guidelines for the multiply injured, multiple amputee. *J Surg Orthop Adv.* 2012 Spring; 21(1):15-21.**

14. Benfield RJ, Mamczak CN, Vo KC, Smith T, Osborne L, Sheppard FR, Elster EA. Initial predictors associated with outcome in injured multiple traumatic limb amputations: A Kandahar-based combat hospital experience. *Injury.* 2012 Jul 25 [E-publication ahead of print].

15. Belmont PJ, Schoenfeld AJ, Goodman G. Epidemiology of combat wounds in operation Iraqi freedom and operation enduring freedom: Orthopaedic burden of disease. *J Surg Orthop Adv* 2010; 19:2-7.

16. Bowyer G. Debridement of extremity war wounds. *J Am Acad Orthop Surg* 2006; 14:S52-56.

17. Mazurek MT, Ficke JR. The scope of wounds encountered in casualties from the Global War On Terrorism: From the battlefield to the tertiary treatment facility. *J Am Acad Orthop Surg* 2006; 14:S18-23.

18. **Institute of Surgical Research, Joint Theater Trauma System CPGs. http://www.usaisr.amedd.army.mil/cpgs/Damage%20Control%20Resuscitation%20-%201%20Feb%202013.pdf.**

19. **http://www.usaisr.amedd.army.mil/cpgs/Fresh_Whole_Blood_Transfusion_24_Oct_12.pdf.**

20. Edens JW, Beekley AC, et al. Long-term outcomes after combat casualty emergency department thoracotomy. *J Am Coll Surg* 2009 Aug; 209(2):188-97.

21. Routt ML Jr, Falicov A, Woodhouse E, et al. Circumferential pelvic antishock sheeting: a temporary resuscitation aid. *J Orthop Trauma* 2002; 16:45–48.

22. Bottlang M, Krieg JC, Mohr M, et al. Emergent management of pelvic ring fractures with use of circumferential compression. *J Bone Joint Surg Am* 2002; 84-A:S43–47.

23. Woods RK, O'Keefe G, Rhee P et al. Open pelvic fracture and colonic diversion. *Arch Surg* 1998; 133:281-86.

24. Osterlee J, McGeehan DF, Robbs JV. Prevention of septic complications in massive pelvic-perineal injuries. *S Afr Med J* 1984; 66:147-150.

25. Davidson BS, Simmons GT, Williamson PR, Buerk CA. Pelvic fractures associated with open perineal wounds: a survivable injury. *J Trauma* 1993; 35:36–39.

26. Serkin FB, Soderdahl DW, Hernandez J, Patterson M et al. Combat urologic trauma in US military overseas contingency operations. *J Trauma* 2010; 69:S175-S178.

27. Epstein RA, Heinemann AW, McFarland LV. Quality of life for veterans and servicemembers with major traumatic limb loss from Vietnam and OIF/OEF conflicts. *J Rehab Res Dev* 2010; 47:373-386.

28. Bumbasirevic M, Lesic A, Mitkovic M, Bumbasirevic V. Delayed wound closure treatment of blast injuries of the extremity. *J Am Acad Orthop Surg* 2006; 14:S77-81.

29. Murray C, Hsu JR, Solomkin JS et al. Prevention and management of infections associated with combat-related extremity injuries. *J Trauma* 2008; 64:S239-251.

30. Haksworth JS, Stojadinovih A, Gage FA, et al. Inflammatory biomarkers in combat wound healing. *Ann Surg* 2009; 250(6):1002-07.

31. Herscovici D Jr, Sanders RW, Scaduto JM, Infante A, DePasquale T. Vacuum-assisted wound closure (VAC therapy) for the management of patients with high-energy soft tissue injuries. *J Orthop Trauma* 2003; 17(10):683-688.

32. Leininger BE, Rasmussen TE, Smith DL, Jenkins DH, Coppola C. Experience with wound VAC and delayed primary closure of contaminated soft tissue injuries in Iraq. *J Trauma* 2006; 61(5):1207-1211.

33. DeCoster TA, Bororgnia S. Antibiotic beads. *J Am Acad Orthop Surg* 2008; 16:674-678.

34. Warner M, Henderson C, Kadrmas W, Mitchell DT. Comparison of vacuum-assisted closure to the antibiotic bead pouch for the treatment of blast injury of the extremity. *Orthop* 2010; 33:77.

35. Anderdson RA, Frisch HM, Farber GL, Hayda RA. Definitive treatment of combat casualties at military medical centers. *J Am Acad Orthop Surg* 2006; 14:S24-S31.

36. **Hunt RC, Kapil V, Basavaraju, SV, et al. National Center for Injury Prevention and Control. Updated in a moment's notice: surge capacity for terrorist bombings. Atlanta, GA: Centers for Disease Control & Prevention, 2010.**

37. Frykberg ER. Medical management of disasters and mass casualties from terrorist bombings: how can we cope? *J Trauma* 2002; 53:201-212.

38. Hunt RC, Ashkenazi I, Falk H. A tale of cities. *Disaster Med Public Health Prep.* 2011; 5: S185-S188.

39. **Butler FK, Blackbourne LH. Battlefield trauma care then and now: A decade of Tactical Combat Casualty Care. *J Trauma Acute Care Surg.* 2012; 73:S395-S402.**

40. Ramasamy A, Hill AM, Clasper JC. Improvised explosive devices: pathophysiology, injury profiles, and current medical management. *J R Army Med Corps.* 2009;155(4):269-272.

41. Rozen N and Dudkiewicz I. Wound ballistics and tissue damage. *Armed Conflict Injuries to the Extremities.* Springer-Verlag, A. Lerner and M. Soudry (eds.). 2011:1-13.

42. Stair RG, Polk DA, Shapiro GL, Tang N. *Law Enforcement Responder, Principles of Emergency Medicine, Rescue, and Force Protection.* Burlington, MA: Jones & Bartlett; 2013.

43. Waxman D. Living with terror, not Living in Terror: The Impact of Chronic Terrorism on Israeli Society. *Perspectives on Terrorism.* Terrorism Research Iniative. 2011; Vol 5, No 5-6.

Additional references/resources—key references/resources have been bolded.

Clinical and Practice Management Resources

- **"Bombings: Injury Patterns and Care," available at http://www.acep.org/blastinjury/**

- **"EMS and Disaster Preparedness," available at http://www.acep.org/disaster/**

- "Blast Injuries: Traumatic Brain Injuries," available at
  http://www.acep.org/uploadedFiles/ACEP/Practice_Resources/disater_and_EMS/disaster_preparedness/
  BlastInjury_Brain%20Injuries_Eng.pdf

- "Bombings: Injury Patterns and Care Pocket Guide," available at
  http://www.acep.org/workarea/downloadasset.aspx?id=33782

- "Coping With a Traumatic Event," available at
  http://media.samhsa.gov/MentalHealth/TraumaticEvent.aspx?from=carousel&position=1&date=3112011

Guidance, Planning and Data Collection Tools

- **"Interim Planning Guidance for Preparedness and Response to a Mass Casualty Event Resulting from Terrorist Use of Explosives," available at http://stacks.cdc.gov/view/cdc/5705**

- **"In a Moment's Notice: Surge Capacity in Terrorist Bombings," available at https://www.facs.org/~/media/files/quality%20programs/trauma/disaster/moments_notice.ashx**

- "Explosions and Blast Injuries: A Primer for Clinicians," available at
  http://www.acep.org/content.aspx?id=43106

- "Medical Record Abstraction Form for Domestic Bombing Events," available at
  http://www.acep.org/uploadedFiles/ACEP/Practice_Resources/disater_and_EMS/Medical%20Record%
  20Abstraction%20Form.pdf

- "Mental Health Survey Instrument," available at
  http://www.cdc.gov/masstrauma/response/mhsurvey_instrument.htm

- "Hospital Disaster Preparedness Self-Assessment Tool," available at
  http://www.acep.org/WorkArea/linkit.aspx?LinkIdentifier=id&ItemID=91205

Endnote References Cited in the Guidance

1. Jacobs LM, McSwain NE Jr, et al. Improving survival from active shooter events: The Hartford Consensus. *J Trauma Acute Care Surg.* 2013 Jun;74(6):1399-1400. http://journals.lww.com/jtrauma/Fulltext/2013/06000/Improving_survival_from_active_shooter_events__.3.aspx.

2. START Global Terrorism Database [database online]. National Consortium for the Study of Terrorism and Responses to Terrorism. http://www.start.umd.edu/start/.

3. Madsen M. Tactical casualty care innovations: News from Iraq. *The Tactical Edge*, Winter 2006:60-68. http://www.chinookmed.com/TheTacticalEdgeMadsenNTOA.pdf.

4. Butler FK Jr, Haymann J, Butler EG. Tactical Combat Casualty Care in Special Operations. *Milit Med.* 1996; 161: 1-16. http://valorproject.org/uploads/TCCC_Special_Operations.pdf.

5. Committee for Tactical Emergency Casualty Care. http://c-tecc.org/.

6. The Committee for Tactical Emergency Care (C-TECC): Evolution and Application of TCCC Guidelines to Civilian High Threat Medicine. *JSOM*, Vol 11, Ed 2;Spring/Summer 2011. https://www.jsomonline.org/PDFs/TECC.pdf

   Joint Committee to Create a National Policy to Enhance Survivability From Mass-Casualty Shooting Events.

7. Improving Survival from Active Shooter Events: The Hartford Consensus. *Bull Am Coll Surg.* 2013;98(6):14-16.

8. Propper BW, Rasmussen TE, Davidson S, et al. Surgical response to multiple casualty incidents in the modern era. *Ann Surg* 2009;250(2):311-315.

9. Ho AM, Karmaker MK, Dion PW. Are we giving enough coagulation factors during major trauma resuscitation? *Am J Surg* 2005;190(3):479-84.

10. Borgman MA, Spinella PC, Perkins J, et al. The ratio of blood products transfused affects mortality in patients receiving massive transfusions at a combat support hospital. *J Trauma* 2007;63(4):805-13.

11. Gonzalez EA, Moore FA, Holcomb JB, et al. Fresh frozen plasma should be given earlier to patients requiring massive transfusion. *J Trauma* 2007;62(1):112-9.

12. Holcomb JB, Wade CE, Michalek JE, et al. Increased plasma and platelet to red blood cell ratios improves outcomes in 466 massively transfused civilian trauma patients. *Ann Surg* 2008;248:447-458.

13. Stein M. Urban bombing: A trauma surgeon's perspective. *Scand J Surg* 2005;94:286–292.

14. Kashuk JL, Halperin P, Caspi G, Colwell C, Moore EE. Evil creativity challenges our trauma systems. *J Am Coll Surg.* 2009 Jul;209(1):134-140.

15. Soffer D, Klausner J, Bar-Zohar D, et al. Usage of blood products in multiple-casualty incidents. The experence of a level I trauma center in Israel. *Arch Surg* 2008; 143(10):983-89.

16. Einav S, Aharonson-Daniel L, Weissman C, et al. In-hospital resource utilization during multiple casualty incidents. *Ann Surg* 2006; 243(4):533-40.

17. Aylwin T, Konig N, Brennan P, et al. Reduction in critical mortality in urban mass casualty incidents: analysis of triage, surge and resource use after the London bombings on July 7, 2005. *Lancet* 2006; (368) 9554:2219- 25.

18. Peleg K, Aharonson-Daniel L, Michael M, et al. Patterns of injury in hospitalized terrorist victims. *Am J Emerg Med* 2003; 21(4):258-62.

19. Turegano-Fuentes F, Caba-Doussoux P, Jover-Navalon J, et al. Injury patterns from major urban terrorist bombings in trains: the Madrid experience. *World J Surg* 2008;32(6):1168-75.

20. Hunt RC, Kapil V, Basavaraju, SV, et al. National Center for Injury Prevention and Control. Updated In A Moment's Notice: Surge Capacity for Terrorist Bombings. Atlanta, GA: Centers for Disease Control and Prevention; 2010. http://emergency.cdc.gov/masscasualties/pdf/surgecapacity.pdf.

21. Schweit KW. Addressing the problem of the active shooter. *FBI Law Enforcement Bulletin*, May 2013. http://www.fbi.gov/stats-services/publications/law-enforcement-bulletin/2013/May/active-shooter.

22. Ergenbright CE, Hubbard SK. Defeating The Active Shooter: Applying Facility Upgrades in Order to Mitigate the Effects of Active Shooters in High Occupancy Facilities. Naval Postgraduate School, June 2012. http://www.ndpci.us/upload/iblock/696/Defeating%20the%20Active%20Shooter.pdf.

23. Morrissey J. EMS Response to Active Shooter Incidents. *EMS World*, July 2011: 42-48. http://emsworld.epubxp.com/i/35512/66.

24. Nordberg M. When kids kill: Columbine High School shooting. *Emergency Medical Services*. Oct1999; 28(10):39-47, 49-50.

25. Mass Shootings at Virginia Tech April 16, 2007, Report of the Virginia Tech Review Panel, August 2007. http://www.governor.virginia.gov/tempcontent/techPanelReport-docs/FullReport.pdf.

26. William H. Webster Commission on The Federal Bureau of Investigation, Counterterrorism Intelligence, and the Events at Fort Hood, Texas, on November 5, 2009. July 12, 2012. http://www.fbi.gov/news/pressrel/press-releases/final-report-of-the-william-h.-webster-commission.

27. Report of the High Level Enquiry Committee (HLEC) on 26/11. Maharashtra Government vide GAD GR No: Raasua. 2008/C.R.34/29-A. http://timesofindia.indiatimes.com/photo/5289981.cms.

28. Shapira S, Hammond J, Cole L. *Essentials Of Terror Medicine*. New York: Springer Science & Business Media; 2009.

29. Caravalho J. Dismounted complex blast injury task force; final report. Prepared for U.S. Army Surgeon General. 18 June 2011:44–47.

30. Eastridge BJ, Mabry R, Seguin P, et al. Prehospital death on the battlefield: implications for the future of combat casualty care. *J Trauma Acute Care Surg* 2012;73:S431-S437.

31. Anderson R, Shawen S, Kragh J, et al: Special topics. *J Am Acad Orthop Surg* 2012;20:S94-S98.

32. Kragh JF Jr, Walters TJ, Baer DG, et al. Practical use of emergency tourniquets to stop bleeding in major limb trauma. *J Trauma* 2008 Feb;64(2 Suppl):S38-49; discussion S49-50.

33. Kheirabadi BS, Scherer MR, Estep JS, Dubick MA, Holcomb JB. Determination of efficacy of new hemostatic dressings in a model of extremity arterial hemorrhage in swine. *J Trauma* 2009 Sep; 67(3):450-9.

34. Kheirabadi B. Evaluation of topical hemostatic agents for combat wound treatment. *US Army Med Dep J.* 2011;Apr-Jun:25-37.

35. National Institute of Justice. Selection and Application Guide to Personal Body Armor. Washington, DC: U.S. Department of Justice; 2001.

36. Montanarelli N, Hawkins CE, Goldfarb MA, Ciurej TF. Protective Garments for Public Officials. Aberdeen Proving Ground, MD: U.S. Army Land Warefare Laboratory;1973.

37. Hanlon E, Gillich P. Origin of the 44-mm Behind-Armor Blunt Trauma Standard. *Military Medicine* 2012;177 (333–339).

38. Montanarelli N, et al. *Protective Garments for Public Officials.*

39. Department of Justice. NILECJ Standard on the Ballistic Resistance of Police Body Armor. Washington, D.C.: U.S. Department of Justice, Law Enforcement Assitance Administration, National Criminal Justice Reference Service; 1972.
———. Supplement I: Status Report to the Attorney General on Body Armor. U.S. Department of Justice Office of Justice Programs National Institute of Justice Safety Initiative Testing and Activities. In Special Report: NIJ; 2004.
———. NIJ Standards: Ballistic Resistance of Body Armor, NIH Standard-0101.06; 2008.

40. Department of Justice. NIJ Standards: Ballistic Resistance of Body Armor, NIH Standard-0101.06; 2008.

41. U.S. Congress, Office of Technology Assessment, *Police Body Armor Standards and Testing, Volume II: Appendices*, OTA-ISC-535. Washington, DC: U.S. Government Printing Office; 1992.

42. National Institute of Justice. Selection and Application Guide to Personal Body Armor. Washington, DC: U.S. Department of Justice; 2001.

43. National Institute of Justice. Standard-0101.06, Ballistic Resistance of Body Armor. https://www.ncjrs.gov/pdffiles1/nij/223054.pdf.

44. Department of Justice. Bulletproof Vest Partnership/ Body Armor Safety Initiative. 2010. http://www.ojp. usdoj.gov/bvpbasi/award_reports/2010vests.html.

45. Salomone JP, Pons PT, McSwain NE. eds. *PHTLS Prehospital trauma life support:Military 7th ed*. St. Louis, MO: Mosby JEMS Elsevier; 2011.